Papists, Protestants and Puritans, 1559–1714

Diana Newton

PUBLISHED BY THE PRESS SYNDICATE OF THE UNIVERSITY OF CAMBRIDGE
The Pitt Building, Trumpington Street, Cambridge CB2 1RP, United Kingdom

CAMBRIDGE UNIVERSITY PRESS
The Edinburgh Building, Cambridge CB2 2RU, United Kingdom
40 West 20th Street, New York, NY 10011–4211, USA
10 Stamford Road, Oakleigh, Melbourne 3166, Australia

First published 1998

Printed in the United Kingdom at the University Press, Cambridge

Typeset in Tiepolo and Formata

A catalogue record for this book is available from the British Library

ISBN 0 521 59845 1 paperback

Text design by Newton Harris Design Partnership

Acknowledgements
All illustrations courtesy of Fotomas Index

Contents

Contents

Introduction

In 1529 the first session of the Reformation Parliament met, and the Reformation in England began. Over the next seven years the links between the English church and Rome – which had existed for more than nine centuries – were formally severed by a series of statutes. By the close of the Reformation Parliament, in 1536, the king (Henry VIII) rather than the pope was the head of the church in England, while legislation aimed at moderate reform of the church was passed. Yet this was not a Protestant Reformation like that on the Continent, which advocated a full-scale attack on the Roman Catholic Church and was to sweep away all things smacking of 'popery'. As the carefully worded Act of Supremacy of 1534 made clear, the king was *acknowledged* and *confirmed* as 'Protector and Supreme Head of the English Church and Clergy so far as the law of Christ allows': he was not *created* as such. It was not until 1552, in the reign of Edward VI, that the first Protestant church service was celebrated. There was a setback under the firmly Catholic Queen Mary, and it was not until 1559, with the Elizabethan Acts of Supremacy and Uniformity, that anything approaching a full Reformation was undertaken, and even that was not comprehensive. In other words, the Reformation in England was much more a 'process' than an 'event'.

This was quite different from the Reformation in Continental Europe. There, complaints against abuses in the church – which had been raised for centuries – suddenly became concentrated into a tenable and widespread reform movement. It was no coincidence that this happened in early sixteenth-century Germany, where the printing process was well advanced. Scholarship burgeoned and old certainties and practices in the church, which seemed to have no proper scriptural (or biblical) basis, were questioned. Most abhorrent was the way in which the Catholic Church claimed to be able to sell to the faithful swift access to heaven. Anti-clericalism, or hostility to the clergy who perpetrated these practices, led to a call by Martin Luther for the abolition of certain Catholic beliefs and practices and a return to Bible-based doctrine. In other words, he protested against the Catholic interpretation of Christianity, which he maintained had become debased over the centuries. Thereafter, Martin Luther, and others of like mind, became known as Protestants.

The Henrician Reformation

King Henry VIII did not approve of Martin Luther and regarded many of his beliefs as heretical. Indeed, he denounced Lutheran teaching in a book entitled *Assertio septem sacramentorum*, which resulted in the pope conferring upon him the title 'Defender of the Faith' in 1521. Thus, the Henrician Reformation presented itself in much more conservative terms. It is possible that, had the pope allowed Henry to divorce his first wife, Catherine of Aragon, in order to marry Anne Boleyn (the affair was known as the king's 'great matter'), there might have been no split with Rome. Certainly, Henry was suspicious of the influence of Continental reformers on the people of England and had some of them burned for disseminating heretical ideas. He justified his position as head of the English church as vital to his overseeing effective action against abuses in the church, a task which the pope was failing to undertake. Yet the most notable episode of reform – the dissolution of the monasteries – was undertaken for financial reasons, though justified on moral grounds. Ostensibly it was intended to close down those monastic communities which had degenerated into ignorance and corruption and to sell their (often substantial) lands to anyone who could afford them. However, it soon became apparent that the process was highly lucrative and beneficial to the crown's financial well-being.

Although Henry had approved the translation of the Bible into English, he was determined that its availability be strictly regulated so that it could not be used to bolster the arguments put forward by those challenging established authority. Right up until the end of his reign, Henry sought to bridle the Reformation of the English church. Not the least of his reasons was his anxiety to prevent new ideas provoking social unrest and disorder. Reformed ideas were attractive – especially to the young and impressionable – for they offered an alternative to traditional values, and they just might stir anti-authoritarian behaviour. In the end, political necessity forced Henry to open the door to Reformation of the English church, but he was highly selective about how much he was prepared to let through.

The Edwardian Reformation

Henry's death and the accession of the young king, Edward VI, in 1547 was seen by some as an opportunity for more radical reform. Thomas Cranmer, archbishop of Canterbury, who had been kept in check by King Henry, was ready to begin the Reformation proper of the English church. Yet his ambitions continued to be frustrated by the essentially conservative outlook of the Lord Protector, the duke of Somerset. Indeed, as with King Henry, Somerset's concern about the church appeared to be driven more by monetary than moral considerations. For example, the Chantries Act, passed in the first year of his Protectorate, ensured a healthy injection of revenue into the exchequer. After Somerset's fall, however, the pace of Reformation quickened and the hopes of the more radical reformers began to be realised. In 1552 Cranmer produced his (second) Book of Common Prayer, which was more uncompromisingly Protestant in its perspective than the first Prayer Book issued in 1547. A second Act of Uniformity (1552), which required that everyone attend church on Sundays to participate in a service according to this new Prayer Book, and no other, ensured its influence would be comprehensive. Then, the following year, the doctrines of the Church of England were registered in the Forty-Two Articles.

By the mid-1540s there was a new influence on the reformers: John Calvin. His outlook, as well as that of a number of other Swiss theologians, was more extreme than the earlier reformers; and they felt that there was still much to be done to complete the Reformation of the church. Calvin's most significant contribution to Protestant thought concerned the matter of predestination. This is the belief that only a limited number of people were destined for eternal salvation and that they were already known to God. These people (i.e. the 'elect') were, like the rest of mankind, essentially sinful, but only they were capable of responding to God's efforts to save them. Everyone else, presumably, was damned. Along with predestination came another unattractive feature of mid-sixteenth-century Protestantism and the Edwardian Reformation. This was the growth of iconoclasm. The fabric of the church – tombs, statues, stained glass windows – together with books deemed heretical, were systematically destroyed. It is difficult to gauge grassroot reaction to such cataclysmic happenings, though historians have recently been making conscientious efforts to do so.

What was certain was that the Reformation depended upon the ability of an unhealthy young man to defy death long enough to allow the reforms of the English church to become firmly ingrained. For his successor was his half-sister, Mary, who had never abandoned her Catholic faith. Efforts to pervert the legitimate succession by having the Protestant Lady Jane Grey proclaimed queen on Edward's death, however, were abortive: clearly, legal considerations outweighed religious sentiments with the English people and Mary was proclaimed queen in 1553, within a month of Edward's death.

The Marian restoration

With the accession of Queen Mary, Catholic hopes were high for a restoration of the old faith and a return to familiar practices in the church. On the Continent the Roman Catholic Church had launched a counter-attack against Protestantism and was endeavouring to set itself in strict order. Accordingly, the Council of Trent was convened in an attempt to effect some kind of reconciliation within Christendom. Although it soon descended into acrimonious theological debate, with any question of compromise with 'condemned heretics' or Protestants abandoned, it did produce a comprehensive definition of Catholic doctrine. With renewed confidence and a change of monarch, English Catholics looked forward to the implementation of the Counter-Reformation in England.

Mary's first parliament duly set about undoing the reforms of her father and brother, and in 1553 the first Act of Repeal was passed, which declared much of Cranmer's work illegal. While support for these moves was not unanimous, in the period after her accession Mary enjoyed much goodwill. Almost immediately, however, she sacrificed it by announcing her intention to marry the king of Spain. It is not clear which most dismayed the English people – the fact that Philip II of Spain was Roman Catholic or that he might regard England as a junior partner of Spain – but a strong tradition was born which equated Englishness with Protestantism. It was to cast a long shadow over foreign relations thereafter.

Ironically, for the first months of her reign, Mary was obliged to conduct religious policy in her capacity as Supreme Head of the English church. However, with the arrival of Cardinal Pole as papal legate to England at the end of 1554, she could return the English church to the custody of the pope. Meanwhile, many of Edward's Protestant bishops either went into exile on the Continent or were deprived of their position or imprisoned and they were replaced by those bishops who had been deprived by Henry VIII. Queen, cardinal and bishops set about reuniting England with the rest of the Roman Catholic Church. At the same time a second Act of Repeal was enacted which rescinded all the statutes which had been passed against Rome since 1529. More worryingly, an Act was passed which revived the heresy laws, which carried with them, as the ultimate punishment for convicted heretics, burning at the stake. While this method of execution did not provoke undue revulsion in the sixteenth century, the scale of its application did, for just under three hundred men and women were burnt for heresy in Mary's reign. As a public relations exercise it was a disaster for the Catholics. Moreover, the Protestant cause was much strengthened by these martyrs, as many moderate Protestants became hardened against Roman Catholicism.

On the other hand, recent research has revealed that the restoration of the Catholic faith was not necessarily arbitrarily imposed on a reluctant populace. The fact that the fabric of the churches could be, and demonstrably was, restored, is testimony to the will of those at parish level to revive Catholic worship. Printing presses, which were perceived as the vehicle for disseminating Protestant ideas, were employed to produce Catholic works, and real efforts were made to improve educational standards among the clergy. All of which belies the traditional view of the Marian church as sterile and arid. But the Catholic restoration could only last as long as Mary lived. When she died, in 1558, followed almost immediately by Cardinal Pole, the Catholic reaction was over.

Ireland

The religious issue in Ireland was less clear-cut than it was in England throughout the sixteenth century. While the Reformation was taking place in England, Henry VIII was endeavouring to extend his political control over Ireland. As part of Irish resistance to these plans, the 'Old English' (descendants of the Anglo-Norman adventurers of the twelfth century, who regarded themselves as the natural rulers of Ireland) appealed to the pope and the Holy Roman Emperor for support against the heretical king of England. However, Henry roundly defeated the rebellion, and an English Lord Deputy was appointed to impose direct English rule over Ireland. Consequently, as the 1536–37 Irish parliament dutifully enacted the legislation of the English Reformation Parliament, it appeared that both clergy and laity accepted Henry VIII's supremacy over the church with few misgivings.

Nevertheless, the doctrinal changes made during Edward VI's reign were unpopular with the Irish, from parish priests to bishops. The majority of the native Irish and the Old English remained committed to Catholicism, whereas the

'New English' (sixteenth-century settlers), who were the most influential group in 1530s Ireland, were identified with Protestantism. In the event, the impact of the Edwardian reforms was negligible, given that little effort was made seriously to impose them on a reluctant populace. Perhaps curiously, the accession of the Catholic Mary Tudor, with the reassuring promise of a return to familiar religious practices, was not greeted with unalloyed joy. For, once again, religious considerations were overshadowed by conflicting family interests within Ireland.

Scotland

As long as the Scottish king, James V, lived, the Roman Catholic Church in Scotland was assured of royal protection against Protestant reformers, and his parliament issued statutes which improved the standing of the church. Nevertheless, the church was always under the authority of the pope. Meanwhile, throughout the 1530s, Scottish Protestants found refuge in England. Then, in 1542, James died and was succeeded by a week-old daughter, Mary (queen of Scots). A proposed marriage between Mary and Prince Edward of England (the future Edward VI) offered hopes to Scottish Protestants. With the end of the 'auld alliance' between Scotland and Catholic France, and Scotland closer to Protestant England, prospects were good for some measure of Protestant reform of the Scottish church. The first step came when the Scottish parliament authorised the reading of scripture in the vernacular (i.e. the native language). But, while the Scottish Protestants welcomed the forthcoming alliance with England, which was to release them from French/Catholic bondage, many Scots were suspicious and fearful of English intentions. Consequently, they vigorously promoted a marriage between Mary and the French dauphin, or heir to the throne. With the French marriage confirmed, the Protestant cause in Scotland was checked, but the Protestants were not eradicated. Led by the radical reformer John Knox, they preached ever more determinedly against Catholicism and the pope.

When Mary Tudor became queen of England, Scottish Catholics felt they had little to fear from the Protestants. Indeed, they were afforded a kind of amused tolerance by the regent of Scotland, Mary's French mother, Mary of Guise. John Knox, in Geneva, might rage against the Catholics, and the French, and female rulers, but essentially he represented an impotent force. Support for Protestantism was prompted more by resistance to the regent and her pro-French policies than by religious or doctrinal considerations. Thus, when five Scottish nobles united in 1557 as the 'First Band of the Lords of the Congregation of Christ' to put down superstitious idolatry (i.e. Roman Catholicism), it was as much to prevent Mary's marriage to the dauphin as for religious purposes.

However, when in 1558 an elderly Protestant was burned for heresy, it seemed to have a similar effect to Mary's burning of heretics in England, in provoking a Protestant backlash. Protestant preachers began to make headway, becoming an increasingly significant force in Scotland. Then, at the end of the year, Mary died. Scottish Catholics no longer had the assurance of a Catholic neighbour. Quite what Scotland did have on her southern border remained to be seen.

The Elizabethan church

Queen Elizabeth was a Protestant. As the product of the king's 'great matter', that was not surprising. But she had also represented the reversionary interests in the reign of Queen Mary – in other words, she became the focus for opponents of Mary's policies, including her religious policy. Elizabeth's commitment to Protestantism was less clear. Her choice of councillors, led by the overtly but pragmatic Protestant William Cecil, indicated that the Reformation of the English church along Protestant lines was to be resumed, while the imminent return of the Protestant exiles ensured that Protestant reform was back on the agenda. Yet Elizabeth herself was a conservative Protestant, while Convocation (the general assembly of the clergy which met at the same time as parliament) and the House of Lords were essentially reactionary in their outlook, which meant that in 1558 there could be no certainties about the future of the English church.

The Elizabethan religious settlement

Nevertheless, in 1559 a religious settlement was constructed which was enshrined in the Acts of Supremacy and Uniformity. The Act of Supremacy was designed to restore royal control over the church and all office-holders were required to take an oath accepting the royal supremacy. The Act of Uniformity imposed consistency in religious or liturgical practice throughout the church in England. This touched every one of the queen's subjects, who were forced to attend their parish church regularly or else face financial penalties. That Elizabeth's view of the church was closer to that of the early Reformation years was demonstrated by her choice of the elderly Matthew Parker as archbishop of Canterbury (1559–75) rather than any of the exiles who were returning from Geneva filled with Calvinist zeal.

In many ways the Elizabethan religious settlement of 1559 was a compromise in that it was intended to turn back the clock to the religious situation as it had been at the death of Edward VI, but with three important concessions to religious conservatives. The first of these concerned the authorised form of worship. Church services were to be conducted according to a new Prayer Book issued in 1558 and based on the 1552 Prayer Book, but with a significant modification to the communion liturgy, that is, the ritual used at the celebration of Holy Communion. Holy Communion, or eucharist, was one of the seven sacraments of the Catholic Church. Others included baptism, marriage and the last rites (prayers said at the moment of death). One of the essential points of conflict between Catholics and Protestants concerned the implications of the communion service, which was observed to honour the broken body and spilt blood of Jesus Christ. Traditionally, the 'communicant' (or worshipper) received from the priest bread and wine which he had transformed into the body and blood of Christ, a process known as transubstantiation. According to Luther, however, the transformation of the bread and wine was a result of the presence of the faithful, rather than any magical powers of the priest – a process which he described as consubstantiation. The 1552 Prayer Book denied both transubstantiation and consubstantiation and, instead, declared that the bread and wine were henceforth to be seen simply as *representing* the body and blood of Christ.

The Elizabethan settlement was designed to accommodate a range of religious convictions. Therefore, the words used during the administration of the eucharist, constituted in the first Edwardian Prayer Book (1549), were added to those of the second Edwardian Prayer Book (1552). Accordingly, as well as enjoining his flock to 'take and eat this in remembrance that Christ died' for them, suggesting a sense of commemoration, the priest had also to assure them that 'the blood of our Lord, Jesus Christ', which was shed for them, would preserve their 'body and soul unto everlasting life', implying a physical presence. In other words, an element of ambiguity was introduced into the precise meaning of the wording used during the administration of the eucharist, which made it acceptable to those from right across the Protestant religious spectrum, for it could be interpreted by each according to their own requirements.

Secondly, all the old 'ornaments of the church and of the ministers' were to be retained. For example, the surplice (a long, white vestment or robe) was to continue as standard wear for the clergy, communicants were allowed to kneel to receive the bread and wine, the sign of the cross was permitted in baptism and the ring could be used in marriage. Furthermore, the directive about further destruction of the fabric of the churches was reassuringly obscure, making the revival of iconoclasm on the scale of the early 1550s less likely. Finally, Elizabeth's title was altered from Supreme Head of the Church to Supreme Governor. Not only did this tackle the knotty question regarding a woman's suitability to lead the church, it also appealed both to Catholics and to the more extreme Protestants. For the former still considered the pope to be head of the church while the latter insisted Jesus Christ was its head.

This, then, was the Elizabethan religious settlement – a compromise which was designed to appeal to as much of the English populace as possible. Yet, almost immediately, its weaknesses were revealed, when all but one of the bishops who were required to take the Oath of Supremacy refused, and they had to be replaced by more accommodating characters. Even so, the church leadership, which was firmly Protestant in outlook, found itself being asked to operate an English church which in many respects was Catholic in nature and did not really reflect recent Protestant theological developments. A commission set up in 1559 to impose the royal supremacy and the Book of Common Prayer onto the clergy was only moderately successful, often achieving nothing more substantial than a grudging and informal submission.

In 1563, Convocation agreed to a series of Articles of Religion which affirmed the 'doctrine of the sacraments' or the beliefs of the Church of England. They became known as the Thirty-Nine Articles of Religion. Although they modified the 1559 settlement to a certain extent, they had not gone far enough for some, and a Puritan element made strenuous efforts to have particular ceremonial observances eliminated by Convocation. They were defeated by just one vote. Typically, Elizabeth left it to her archbishop of Canterbury, Matthew Parker, to enforce conformity. In 1565 he issued a series of moderate requirements from the clergy – the *Book of Advertisements* – which served only to harden the resolve of the more extreme Puritans. The Thirty-Nine Articles were confirmed by statute (i.e. enacted by parliament) in 1571. On the other hand, attempts to impose a revival of iconoclasm were also only partially effective because, in many parish churches, Catholic paraphernalia was merely locked away, presumably in case it was needed later.

Varieties of Protestant belief

At first it was believed by many that the 1559 settlement was only a temporary measure, to be further developed and expanded upon in due course. As the Marian exiles returned home to continue the reform of the English church (which had been interrupted by Mary's efforts to restore the Catholic faith), it became clear that the years they had spent in and around Geneva had exposed them to a set of thoughts and beliefs which were quite different from those of Elizabeth and some of her closest advisers. In 1560 the Geneva Bible was published in England and the more radical Protestants sought to construct an English church on the Genevan model, which removed authority from the bishops and gave it to local and general assemblies staffed by representatives elected by members of the congregation. This system of church government became known as 'Presbyterianism', while the advocates of further reform, or purification, of the church and society were called 'Puritans' (often disparagingly).

Puritans adopted Calvinist thinking almost unreservedly. They were firmly committed to Calvin's doctrine of predestination and, in order to facilitate the advancement of the 'elect', devoted a large proportion of their time to religious activities, either in private prayer or pursuing 'religious exercises'. These included assembling to read the Bible, attending lectures on subjects of a religious nature and deliberating over religious matters at meetings called 'prophesyings'. While ostensibly organised as a consequence of the shortage of preachers, these gatherings were viewed with suspicion by the queen, who saw in them a challenge to her 1559 settlement. The moderate Puritan Edmund Grindal, archbishop of Canterbury from 1575, on the other hand, was convinced that religious exercises were essential for the future health of the church and he risked incurring royal displeasure by defending them. The Puritans lost valuable support when Grindal was succeeded at Canterbury by John Whitgift, in 1583, for his position was much closer to Elizabeth's regarding Puritan nonconformity.

Meanwhile, the Puritans endeavoured to create God's kingdom on earth by preparing society for the return of Christ and God's final judgement on his creation. As well as ministers filling a fatherly corrective role, civil authorities also had their part to play. Thus, the Puritan clergy supported the efforts of the gentry in their capacity as local magistrates (Justices of the Peace or JPs) and members of parliament to impose discipline. But, while this commitment to effecting an orderly society was commendable, the habit of Puritans to gather together to engage in 'religious exercises' (at 'conventicles') provoked misgivings on the part of the state. Their clear dissatisfaction with the religious settlement of 1559, and their determination to further cleanse the church of Catholic influences, reinforced the reputation of Puritans as potential subversives.

Nevertheless, the Puritans were always committed to further reform of the English church from within. They were even willing to work with an episcopacy (church government by bishops) if it were necessary. There were others who felt that a true Bible-based church could only be achieved apart and separate from the established church with its ecclesiastical hierarchy, which they believed to be contrary to the word of God. Accordingly, in the 1580s, they set up separate communities – such as the Brownists, who were followers of Robert Browne (?1550–?1633), and the members of the Family of Love, or Familists – and set about restoring the church according to its biblical origins. Because these separatists were clearly divisive and threatened the unity of the realm – at a time when a united realm was essential to its well-being – they were perceived by the authorities as subversive. In extreme cases, some of their leaders were executed on charges of sedition. In general, though, their activities tended to be on the fringes of society and, by maintaining a low profile, they avoided attracting undue persecution by the state.

Finally, there was a Protestant element which was, by and large, content with the religious settlement. But because satisfied customers are not usually as vociferous as malcontents, they tend to be less easy to observe. These Protestants have been described as 'Anglicans' or as 'Prayer Book Protestants', suggesting a sincere attachment to the form of service and ceremonial as advocated by the 1559 Book of Common Prayer. Whether their quiescence was indicative of their sincere accord with the church as it was established in 1559, or was simply a manifestation of apathy or indifference, is difficult to determine, but they seem to have represented a significant proportion of the English population. Moreover, the traditional view of the Elizabethan church as a battleground, with the 'Anglican' establishment under constant challenge from a Puritan opposition, has probably been overdrawn. The situation was more one of different emphases over the need for further Reformation of the church. So that while, on occasion, conflicts did spring up and attract considerable attention, at other times the church was relatively quiet.

Roman Catholics and church Papists

Catholic survival into Elizabeth's reign has been the subject of much debate among historians. One view maintains that the Catholic community survived from Mary's reign, depending on their priests to ensure that Catholic practices quietly endured in the households of the Catholic gentry. The other view is that Catholicism was revived in the 1570s as part of a conscious mission when newly qualified priests from foreign seminaries (training colleges for Catholic priests) secretly infiltrated English gentry households.

English Catholics in the reign of Elizabeth adopted one of two courses. Some, known as 'church Papists', outwardly conformed to Protestantism by attending church services often enough to avoid prosecution. They justified their decision either by stressing their desire not to break the law or else by maintaining that by being selective they could, in conscience, attend ordinary Sunday services without compromising their beliefs. Moreover, by deflecting the attention of the authorities and adopting church papistry, many Catholics actually ensured the continuity of Catholicism, because protecting their estates from confiscation by the law meant they were then able to maintain priests to perpetuate the practice of their faith. Other Catholics, however, refused to attend authorised church services under any circumstances and suffered the consequences. Laws were passed, in 1581 and 1585, making 'recusancy' (refusal to attend church services according to the settlement of 1559) punishable by hefty fines and the confiscation of lands, which could cripple a Catholic family. This was a far cry from the 1559 Act of Uniformity, which had imposed a fine of twelve pence (5p) for each absence from church. Some Catholics worked out a compromise whereby the head of a household attended church services to avoid the full rigour of the law while the rest of the family adopted the stricter recusant position.

Tensions within the Elizabethan church 1: the Puritans

The first major controversy in the Elizabethan church concerned clerical dress. As part of Elizabeth's determination to enforce conformity she directed her archbishop of Canterbury, Matthew Parker, to issue an order for all clergymen to wear a surplice when conducting church services and the traditional everyday dress at all other times. (This was one of the directions in Parker's 1565 *Book of Advertisements*.) However, for many people the prescribed vestments were too closely associated with Roman Catholicism and the celebration of mass. Worse, there was no biblical precedent regarding clerical dress. The issue threatened to polarise the English church, with the more radical Puritan element insisting they would not revert to discredited Catholic practices, while the more moderate bishops, required to enforce a ruling they felt was one of several 'matters indifferent', reluctantly endeavoured to comply with the queen's wishes. There were riots on the streets of London, a furious pamphleteering contest ensued, and a number of ministers were deprived of their livings. In the end the

Vestments Controversy was resolved in the queen's favour – but it was an uneasy victory and was only ever partially enforceable.

One outcome of the Vestments Controversy was a hardening of Puritan attitudes. The late 1560s saw a new generation of Puritans led by Thomas Cartwright, a young Cambridge Professor, who demanded that the English church be restructured along the lines of Calvin's church in Geneva – that is, on Presbyterian lines, and without bishops. Under pressure from William Cecil and John Whitgift (Master of Trinity College, Cambridge, later archbishop of Canterbury), Cartwright was expelled from Cambridge and he left for Geneva in December 1570. But the Puritan struggle continued. It was reinforced by the support of Puritan gentry who sat in the House of Commons as MPs, and in the 1571 session they introduced a Bill to reform the Prayer Book. With renewed confidence, Cartwright returned and engaged in a pamphlet war with Whitgift. However, the moderate Puritans were unnerved by the position adopted by the more radical reformers, and they reasserted their leadership. Prospects looked even more promising for effecting further reform of the English church – from within the system – when Edmund Grindal was appointed archbishop of Canterbury in 1575.

Grindal, however, soon came into conflict with Elizabeth – and her view that the church had been sufficiently reformed – over the matter of Puritan 'prophesyings'. Although he could not be dismissed, he was suspended from office by the queen in 1577 and it seemed that moderate Puritan ambitions were never to be achieved. On his death in 1583 he was succeeded by Whitgift. Although Whitgift appeared to be much more in tune with the queen than his predecessor, he still had ambitions to reform the church at certain levels. His principal concern was ending abuses against the church, especially regarding church property and finances. While these were not as blatant as under Henry VIII and Edward VI, the church was still exploited by the laity, who pocketed the profits from vacant bishoprics and impropriated tithes (i.e. they took for themselves money and lands which rightfully belonged to the church). As the chief culprits were the queen and her principal subjects, he had to tread carefully.

Accordingly he set out to work with Convocation to address the question of lay interference in church affairs as part of a package of reform of church (especially clerical) standards in general. The central tenet of his initiative was to enforce complete conformity among the clergy, embodied in instructions for all ministers formally to subscribe to a declaration that the Prayer Book 'contains nothing contrary to the word of God'. In the face of opposition from a number of privy councillors, he modified his direction with an *ex officio* oath. In other words, by virtue of his office, any member of the clergy was obliged to explain his beliefs on demand. This did not lessen unease with Whitgift, however, and he found himself in conflict with William Cecil (now Lord Burghley) and other powerful councillors.

Meanwhile the Puritans were again gathering force. After the 1583 session of parliament – when Elizabeth had resorted to her powers as Supreme Governor of the church to thwart their attempts to use the parliamentary process to effect further reform of the church – the Puritan leaders concentrated their efforts on the session of parliament which was to meet in 1586. They produced a report on the clergy which revealed that educational standards were as low as ever, and initiated a drive to correct abuses against the church and improve the standards of the clergy. This was to be based on a *Book of Discipline*, which set out how a Presbyterian system of church government would be organised. Elizabeth simply reasserted that parliamentary intervention in the government of the church was contrary to the royal prerogative.

With their hopes for reforming the church from within dashed, in the late 1580s the radical Puritans embarked on a campaign of denouncing the established church through a series of vitriolic dispatches called the *Marprelate Letters*. This finally gave the authorities the justification they needed to act against the Puritans: their leaders were imprisoned in 1591 and some were executed in 1593. Thereafter, though they were never completely suppressed in the regions, where they still commanded the support of many of the gentry, the Puritans were sufficiently subdued at the centre no longer to represent a viable challenge to the established church. Possibly they felt that, with the queen getting older, their best hopes for realising their ambitions lay in the future.

Tensions within the Elizabethan church 2: the Catholics

During the first decade of Elizabeth's reign, the Catholics were relatively tractable. The religious settlement was not as unacceptable as it might have been – although a number of Marian bishops had been deprived of their office in 1559 – and it was possible for Catholics to maintain a low profile throughout the 1560s while quietly continuing to worship according to Catholic rites, especially in areas remote from the capital. Catholics who could not accept the English church as it was established in 1559 went into exile. But then, in 1570, Pope Pius V issued the Bull (i.e. decree) *Regnans in excelsis*, which excommunicated Elizabeth and released her Catholic subjects from loyalty to her. It was a short step to Roman Catholicism becoming perceived as the religion of disloyalty, and its association with foreign aggression, born in the reign of Queen Mary, was revived. By the same token, Protestantism became synonymous with patriotism.

The Catholic menace was also present closer to home. In 1569 there was a rising of the northern Catholic earls, who felt increasingly out of sympathy with the English government. Though the Northern Rising did not attract large-scale support from the English Catholics, and it was easily put down, it did demonstrate a certain danger from within the realm. That the Northern Rising had tenuous links with the queen of Scots and the king of Spain, which were strengthened for the second rebellion against Elizabeth in 1571 (the so-called Ridolfi Plot), was a clear indication that firm action was needed against the Catholics. Accordingly, the parliament of 1572 responded with the first of a series of Acts against the Catholic community. Throughout the remainder of Elizabeth's reign, anti-Catholic legislation became increasingly severe to counter the growing threat posed by the Catholics, especially when they were bolstered by the Jesuits.

The defcription of the burning of Thomas Haukes in Effex,
at a towne called Coxehall. Anno. 1555. the. 10. of Iune.

John Foxe's *Actes and monuments*, published in 1563, contrasts devout Protestants, prepared to die for their faith, with self-indulgent Catholics, preoccupied with ritual at the expense of personal piety. Given that the book was also known as 'Foxe's book of martyrs', how might it have been exploited by Protestants in their struggle against Catholicism, then and subsequently?

Among the Catholics who left England after the death of Queen Mary in 1558 were over a hundred Oxford graduates. Led by William Allen, a number of them founded a college (or seminary) for young Englishmen at Douai, in the Spanish Netherlands, where Catholic learning could flourish. Though it was not originally intended to serve any other purpose, a steady stream of its graduates (i.e. seminary priests) returned to England to strengthen the Catholic cause throughout the 1570s. Then they joined forces with priests from the English College at Rome, run by the Society of Jesus (the Jesuits), who were passionately committed to missionary endeavour. This Jesuit campaign was to be organised far more effectively than recent efforts had been, and in 1580, under the leadership of Robert Parsons and Edmund Campion, they arrived in England. Despite its declared intention not to become involved in English politics, the mission was identified with papal interests, and the pope was in conflict with Elizabeth.

Elizabeth's parliaments of 1581 and 1585 passed increasingly repressive legislation against both Catholic recusants and missionary priests. Fines for failing to attend church services escalated from a shilling a month to twenty pounds, and failure to pay could result in the exchequer sequestering two-thirds of the recusant's lands. Missionary priests were subject to execution by hanging, drawing and quartering, and over a hundred of them paid the penalty, including Campion. Many Catholics wanted to declare their allegiance to the queen in order to secure a relaxation of her government's persecution and to be allowed quietly to practise their faith. They also wished to escape from Jesuit influence, with its commitment to returning England to papal control. This division among the Catholics ensured that, by the end of Elizabeth's reign in 1603, the impact of the Catholic mission was mitigated. But it was never eliminated, for in 1602 the pope had appointed an archpriest to take control of the mission. Clearly, the Catholics as well as the Puritans had an eye to a future after Queen Elizabeth.

Document case study

1.1 Parliament legislates to ensure compulsory attendance at church and conformity in church services

Extract from the Act for the Uniformity of Common Prayer and Divine Service in the Church, and the Administration of the Sacraments, 1559

III. . . . from [24 June] all . . . persons inhabiting within this realm . . . shall diligently and faithfully, having no lawful or reasonable excuse to be absent, endeavour themselves to resort to their parish church or chapel accustomed, or . . . to some usual place where Common Prayer and such service of God shall be used . . . upon every Sunday, and other days ordained and used to be kept as Holy Days, and then and there to abide orderly and soberly, during the time of the Common Prayer, Preachings or other Service of God there to be used and ministered; upon pain of punishment by the censures of the Church, and also upon pain that every person so offending shall forfeit for every such offence twelve pence, to be levied by the church-wardens of the parish where such offence shall be done, to the use of the poor of the same parish . . .

Source: *The statutes of the realm,* 12 vols., London, 1810–18, vol. IV. i, pp. 356–57

1.2 Legislation denying papal authority

Part of the Act for the Assurance of the Queen's Majesty's Royal Power over all Estates and Subjects within her Highness' Dominions, 1563

. . . if any person . . . shall by writing . . . preaching or teaching, deed or act . . . maintain or defend the authority, jurisdiction or power of the bishop of Rome [i.e. the pope], or of his see, heretofore claimed, used or usurped within this realm . . . or by any speech, open deed or act, advisedly and wittingly attribute any such manner of jurisdiction, authority or preeminence to the said see of Rome . . . then every such person . . . shall incur the . . . penalties provided by the Statute of Provision and Præmunire[*] . . .

---

[*] a penalty of outlawry (i.e. loss of the monarch's protection and the benefit of the law) and forfeiture (i.e. loss of lands and/or goods) according to an Act of 1392

Source: *Statutes of the realm,* vol. IV. i, pp. 402–03

1.3 Legislation to counter the first wave of Catholic missionaries

Part of the Act against the Bringing in and Putting in Execution of Bulls and other Instruments from the See of Rome, 1571

IV. . . . if any person shall . . . bring into this realm of England . . . any crosses, pictures, beads or such-like vain and superstitious things, from the Bishop or see of Rome . . . and divers pardons, immunities and exemptions granted by the authority of the said see . . . and if the same person so bringing in as aforesaid such . . . other things as before specified . . . shall deliver . . . the same . . . to be used or worn in any wise . . . shall incur the penalties ordained by the Statute of Præmunire and Provision* . . .

_____
* see above

Source: *Statutes of the realm,* vol. IV. i, pp. 529–30

1.4 Legislation forbidding Catholic recusants to say and hear mass

Part of the Act to Retain the Queen's Majesty's Subjects in their Due Obedience, 1581

I. . . . That all persons . . . which . . . shall by any ways or means put in practice to . . . withdraw any of the Queen's Majesty's subjects . . . from their natural obedience to her Majesty, or to withdraw them for that intent from the religion now by her Highness' authority established . . . to the Romish religion, or to move them to promise any obedience to any pretended authority of the See of Rome, or of any other prince, state or potentate . . . shall be adjudged to be traitors, and . . . shall . . . suffer and forfeit as in case of high treason . . .

III. . . . every person which shall say or sing mass . . . shall forfeit the sum of 200 marks* and be committed to prison . . . there to remain by the space of one year . . .

IV. . . . every person above the age of sixteen years, which shall not repair to some church, chapel or usual place of common prayer . . . shall forfeit to the Queen's Majesty, for every month . . . £20 of lawful English money

_____
* 1 mark = 13 shillings and four pence, or around 67p

Source: *Statutes of the realm,* vol. IV. i, p. 657

1.5 Legislation declaring Jesuits and other Catholic missionaries illegal

Part of the Act against Jesuits, Seminary Priests and such other like Disobedient Persons , 1585

II. . . . It shall not be lawful for any Jesuit, seminary priest or other . . . ecclesiastical person . . . ordained . . . by any authority derived . . . from the See of Rome . . . to come into or remain in any part of this realm . . . and every person which . . . shall wittingly and willingly . . . aid or maintain any such Jesuit [etc.] . . . shall . . . for such offence be adjudged a felon, without benefit of clergy, and suffer death and forfeit as in case of one attainted of felony.

Source: *Statutes of the realm,* vol. IV. i, p. 706

Document case-study questions

The questions are based on the documents but you may need to look elsewhere in the book for relevant information.

1 Why was such importance attached to enforcing religious uniformity in England after the accession of Elizabeth (1.1)?

2 What conclusions can be drawn from 1.2 about political attitudes towards Roman Catholicism and the pope?

3 According to the piece of legislation in 1.3, what did Elizabeth's government perceive as particularly threatening to security? What had prompted them to identify examples of Roman Catholic subversion?

4 How were attitudes against Roman Catholicism seen to be hardening after 1581 (1.4)? Why?

5 Why was it necessary to enact still more stringent legislation against Catholic recusants (1.5)?

6 What are the principal motives underlying religious legislation in the reign of Queen Elizabeth?

2 The religious context of England's foreign relations in the late sixteenth century

Sixteenth-century Europe was dominated by religious issues in which England was embroiled, to a greater or lesser degree, throughout the period. In the early years France posed the greatest threat to England but when France was almost torn apart by religious wars in the 1560s, Habsburg Spain became the principal Catholic power in Europe. With the marriage between King Philip of Spain and Queen Mary of England, England found herself dragged into the war between France and Spain. Even after the death of Mary, when Spain no longer had any direct influence on English affairs, Spain continued to preoccupy England. This was most marked after 1572, when Spanish troops were sent to crush the rebellious Calvinists in the Low Countries (or Netherlands, i.e. modern-day Holland and Belgium), who were looking for independence from Spain. Elizabeth was wooed by the French (literally as well as metaphorically) to join them in an anti-Habsburg league. When Elizabeth was reluctantly drawn into the conflict, in support of the Protestant Dutch, she found herself in a prolonged dispute which would prove to be a massive drain on her annual revenue and was to continue for the rest of her life.

Meanwhile, Elizabeth had problems closer to home. Ireland sought greater independence from England by means of a series of rebellions which were often sustained by Spanish arms, men and money. Then, in the 1590s, the Ulster earls – once again with Spanish support – engaged England in a prohibitively expensive war which was also to last until the end of Elizabeth's reign. In addition, the Catholic queen of Scots fled Protestant Scotland and sought the protection of her cousin Elizabeth. For almost twenty years she lived at Elizabeth's expense while providing a focus for English and foreign Catholic ambitions – ambitions which, on occasion, included the elimination of Elizabeth.

Ireland

Elizabeth inherited an Ireland which, by and large, was loyal to the crown, and there was a climate of goodwill between her government and the native lords. However, the Irish were generally unresponsive to her Protestant religious settlement (see above, pp. 7–8), even though it had been slightly watered down to make it more appropriate for Ireland. The main difficulty for those seeking reform was that the church in Ireland suffered from poor organisation and an under-educated clergy. Though strenuous efforts were made to overcome these problems, they were only partially successful and hopes for implementing reform were pinned on the New English settlers, who were predominantly Protestant. It was expected that they would exercise an evangelising influence in their communities. For the present, an informal toleration of Catholics prevailed, and conciliation and co-operation rather than confrontation seemed to be the order of the day.

However, the atmosphere changed after Elizabeth was excommunicated by the pope in 1570. Ever since England's break with Rome in the 1530s, the most militant Irish Catholics had regularly appealed to Spain for their help to resist further domination by the English. They emphasised the advantages to an enemy of England in coming to an understanding with England's close neighbour, and Spain was happy to exploit any situation which might challenge English power. But even with Spanish support and papal encouragement, the Irish rebels never achieved very much. The first disastrous campaign of 1580 was followed by further defeats and, as a consequence, English royal power increased throughout the 1580s and 1590s.

Then, in 1593, a confederacy of bishops and lords from the north of Ireland – led by the earls of Tyrone and Tyrconnel and the archbishop of Armagh – once again solicited Spanish assistance against England, arguing that both the cause of religion and Spanish interests would be served. But Spain was already fully stretched with its wars against both France and the Dutch rebels, and it was not until the summer of 1599 that the Spanish king sent any arms to Ireland. The Spanish Council of State emphasised the advantages of engaging England in an Irish war, by pointing out that it would counter Elizabeth's assistance to Spain's rebellious subjects in the Low Countries.

The Nine Years War, which broke out in 1594, was fought ostensibly to restore Catholicism to Ireland but it was also envisaged, by some, that English authority would be replaced by Spanish power – the Nine Years War was a typical example of the politico-religious nature of sixteenth-century diplomacy. It was a prohibitively expensive campaign and an unremitting drain on the English exchequer, until peace was imposed on the rebels in 1603. They were forced to surrender to Elizabeth's Lord Deputy, Mountjoy, though when O'Neill, earl of Tyrone, submitted, Elizabeth had been dead for almost a week, a detail which had been concealed from him. In fact, he had surrendered to King James VI of Scotland and I of England.

Scotland

King James VI was the son of Mary, queen of Scots, who in 1558, the year of Elizabeth's accession, was living in France, married to the dauphin, the heir to the French throne. She was to become queen of France the following year and, in the meantime, had declared herself to be the rightful (and Catholic) queen of England. In Mary's absence, Scotland was ruled by Mary's mother, Mary of Guise, acting as regent. After the death of the Catholic Mary Tudor in 1558, Scotland once again found herself with a Protestant neighbour. Greatly encouraged, the leading Protestant John Knox returned from exile and the

Scottish Protestants prepared to effect a Reformation of the Scottish church. In 1559 a confederation of Protestant nobles – or Lords of the Congregation – challenged the competence of the regent. In October 1559 they deposed her, ostensibly in the name of Queen Mary. In the same year they signed the Treaty of Berwick with England, which ensured English support for their cause. France, on the other hand, was preoccupied by her own religious conflicts and unable to send any more troops to Scotland. When Mary of Guise died in 1560, the way was clear for another treaty – the Treaty of Edinburgh – which provided for both England and France to withdraw from Scotland. The treaty also provided for a meeting of the Scottish parliament.

This was to be the Scottish Reformation Parliament, which achieved in three weeks what had taken the English Reformation Parliament seven years. By passing just three Acts, the whole base of the pre-Reformation church was dismantled. Soon after, a Confession of Faith was produced which set out Protestant doctrine in wholly positive (rather than negative anti-Papist) terms. With their queen still in France (where she remained for a further fourteen months), the outcome of the Reformation Parliament was quietly adopted by Scotland. Kirk sessions (i.e. church meetings to impose ecclesiastical discipline) were set up after 1560 and became the local basis for the reorganised Scottish church. The Protestants had achieved the Reformation of Scottish religion.

When Mary did finally return to rule Scotland in August 1561 she did nothing to reverse the Reformation in Scotland, though she insisted on practising the Catholic faith herself. Jesuits arriving from the Continent were greeted by a demoralised and despairing Catholic community. Mary further confused the issue by seeking to make a Catholic marriage, originally within one of the great Catholic royal houses of France or Spain. But hopes that this might be a precursor to reversing the Protestant Reformation in Scotland were dashed in 1565 when she finally married the half-heartedly Catholic Henry, Lord Darnley, who was as reluctant as Mary to further the Catholic cause in Scotland.

Then, when Mary eventually began to adopt a pro-Catholic policy in the summer of 1565, it was too late and woefully inadequate. If anything, her position was even more confused. She appointed more Catholics to sit on her privy council and she resumed relations with the pope, but her increasing dependence on foreign advisers simply antagonised the Protestants. When she forced the issue by engaging in a show of strength with the Protestant Lords, she lost, whereupon she revived friendly relations with England and her efforts on behalf of the Catholics ceased. Indeed, after the murder of Darnley (in which Mary was implicated) she married the earl of Bothwell by Protestant rites. In June 1567 Mary was forced to abdicate and her 13-month-old son was crowned James VI of Scotland: the name James, in preference to Charles (as he had been baptised), with its Catholic connotations, was deemed more suitable for one who would rule over a Protestant Scotland.

Knox and the Protestants consolidated their position as they sought to establish what the Puritans were endeavouring to achieve in England – a radical Protestant church. Already a Presbyterian system of church government was in place, with local assemblies answerable to regional synods and then to one national body (or General Assembly). After the death of Knox in 1572, a new wave of Calvinists returned from Geneva, including Andrew Melville, who published a *Book of Discipline* which declared that the church was quite separate from, and superior to, the state. Melville claimed that there were two kingdoms and that King James was but a subject in the Kingdom of Jesus Christ the King. This was a direct challenge to the lay ruler (the king), whose parliament responded by passing the so-called 'Black Acts' in 1584, which brought the church back firmly under royal control.

For the rest of his time in Scotland James was engaged in retaining his influence on the Scottish church by means of encouraging the moderate element and taking personal control of the General Assembly. By detaching the radicals from the mainstream he was able to marginalise and neutralise them. At the same time he was also determined to maintain his authority over the Catholic earls, who were a potential threat to the stability of Scotland. On the other hand he was not disposed to persecute loyal subjects for their religious beliefs and he steadfastly resisted demands from the kirk that he act against the Catholics. James's handling of the two issues was, on the whole, effective. It was an approach he was to continue when he became James I of England, as well as James VI of Scotland, in 1603.

France

The traditional enmity between France and England was intensified by the addition of the religious factor in the sixteenth century. Henry VIII's wars against France in the 1540s were financed, in part, by the proceeds of the dissolution of the monasteries, and even Mary Tudor's programme of restoring property to the church was frustrated by the costs of another war with France (1557–59), a war during which England famously lost Calais. When Elizabeth succeeded Mary to the English throne she found herself at war with France, which, given their links, meant she was also at war with Scotland. It was not until England was at peace that Elizabeth felt free to proceed with restoring the Protestant church, and, in the spring of 1559, peace was concluded between France and Spain by the Treaty of Cateau-Cambrésis, which included England and Scotland. If peace enabled Elizabeth to devote herself to settling religion in England, it also gave the French monarchy the opportunity to tackle its own religious problems, which principally concerned the challenge to the Catholic faith posed by the Calvinist Huguenots. Its first act was savagely to punish the ringleaders of a Huguenot 'conspiracy' at Amboise.

Meanwhile, France continued until 1561 to be the residence of Mary, queen of Scots, who claimed to be the rightful queen of England. It was a situation which France intended to exploit fully, not least in ensuring that England was rescued from a heretical queen and restored to the Catholic faith. However, France was about to be engulfed in a series of hideous internal wars of religion which lasted throughout the 1560s and 1570s, diverting attention from both Scotland and

England. Even so, Mary's failure to restore the Catholic faith to Scotland after her return was viewed with dismay by the French, though her marriage to the ostensibly Catholic Darnley in 1565 was welcomed. By the time it was clear that Catholic expectations were premature, and Mary had fled to England (1567), France was immersed in a second round of religious wars. In any case, Mary had by this stage lost all credibility with the Catholic powers on the Continent. France was now in competition with England for control of the young King James VI, and was no longer interested in Mary. During her 19 years in England it was Spain, not France, who became involved in the series of intrigues and plots to replace Elizabeth with Mary.

After Mary's abdication, French interest in England was centred on persuading the English to join a league against Habsburg Spain. It was even proposed that Elizabeth might marry the duke of Anjou, brother of the French king, Henri III. This alliance was to form part of a coalition with the Protestant rebels in the Low Countries and it was an example of what was to become a French dilemma: while adhering to a Catholic policy at home, she was obliged to pursue a Protestant foreign policy. Elizabeth declined Anjou's offer of marriage – either because she wished to retain her bargaining power as a potential partner or because she had no intention of promoting the interests of France. However, after the assassination of Henri III by a Catholic fanatic in 1589, she was prepared to become involved in French matters when she supported the Protestant Henri of Navarre to secure the crown of France, which she did to the tune of several thousand English men and many thousands of pounds. No doubt she was also anxious to ensure that France was not ruled by a pro-Spanish king, for Spain was vehemently opposed to Henri of Navarre, and Elizabeth's foreign policy was grounded upon playing off the Spanish against the French.

Henri IV was to bring to an end the French wars of religion. But it was only after his discovery that 'Paris was worth a mass', and his decision to renounce his Protestant faith and embrace Catholicism, that he was in a position to assume full control of France. Thereafter, he allowed the Huguenots to practise their religion undisturbed and to control a number of important cities and strongholds. The generous terms were enshrined in the Edict of Nantes, issued in 1598 – the year that Philip, king of Spain, died.

Spain

The marriage of Philip of Spain to Mary Tudor in 1554 was viewed with suspicion by English Protestants, but for English Catholics it offered hopes of a Catholic dynasty which would ensure that the religious events in the reigns of Henry VIII and Edward VI were simply a temporary aberration in the history of a Catholic England. But Mary died childless. Philip actually contemplated marrying Elizabeth to retain his influence over England but it was an unrealistic ambition; Elizabeth was too closely identified with Protestant hopes and Philip too uncompromising a champion of Catholicism. Nevertheless, relations between England and Spain remained, necessarily, cordial.

Then, in 1567, the relationship was threatened by two developments. The first concerned the revolt in the Low Countries against their Spanish overlords, and the second was the arrival in England of Mary, queen of Scots. Initially the rebels in the Netherlands consisted of both Catholics and Protestants and their motivation was commercial rather than ideological. However, Philip's efforts to impose Catholic doctrines on the Lutheran and Calvinist elements in the Netherlands – backed by the rigour of the Inquisition (a special court to deal with heresy, and especially Protestant heresy) – stiffened the resolve of the more extreme Protestants, who were determined to free themselves from Spanish domination. Elizabeth was reluctantly involved in the struggle because a number of Calvinist privateers from Zeeland and Holland, in the Low Countries, were using English ports as bases for their operations. Under pressure from the Spanish, she ordered them to leave but she warned Philip that sooner or later England would be obliged to intervene in the Low Countries.

Relations between England and Spain were further strained by the presence in England of Mary, queen of Scots, who continued to offer herself in marriage to anyone who would support her claim to the English throne and thus ensure the restoration of Catholicism to England. While not offering marriage, the king of Spain was prepared to join the English Catholics who were intriguing and plotting to replace Elizabeth with Mary. The first of these plots was connected with the rising of the northern earls against Elizabeth and her government in 1569, which was put down relatively easily, though at great cost to the more humble of the rebels, around 450 of whom lost their lives (see above, p. 12). In 1571 the leaders of the Northern Rising, together with the Spanish ambassador and a Florentine banker called Ridolfi (who was also an agent of the pope), conspired to incite the English Catholics to rebellion and, with the support of a Spanish army, to capture Elizabeth and release Mary. The scheme was discovered, however, and its English leader, the duke of Norfolk, was executed in 1572. The Spanish continued to support Mary in conspiracies against Elizabeth, the most notable being the Throckmorton Plot (1583) and the Babington Plot (1586). The discovery of a letter from Mary to the young English Catholic Anthony Babington, fully endorsing the murder of Elizabeth, finally prompted the English queen to sign Mary's death warrant. She was executed in February 1587. Thereafter, the king of Spain's daughter became the chief Catholic claimant to the English throne.

Meanwhile, in 1585 Elizabeth had openly intervened in the Low Countries on behalf of the Protestant rebels in the northern provinces. Relations between Spain and England were steadily deteriorating and, in the summer of 1588, Philip launched his 'enterprise of England' or Armada to conquer England, which would herald a restoration of the Catholic faith. Although traditionally the English victory was broadcast as the triumph of 'right' against 'might', the two sides were fairly evenly matched. The importance of the English defeat of the Spanish Armada lies more in its propaganda factor, for it allowed Elizabeth to pose as the Protestant bulwark against Roman Catholic Spain. Anti-Spanish sentiments, deliberately whipped up once war with Spain seemed unavoidable, were rooted in anti-Papist feeling. The English were firmly ranged on the side of the Dutch Calvinists, to the approval of the Protestants (and especially the Puritans) in England.

The Low Countries

The Low Countries were part of the Spanish empire in the sixteenth century. They consisted of a confederation of provinces which were prosperous and commercially successful. The reforming ideas of Luther and later Calvin were embraced enthusiastically by a significant proportion of the population, especially in the northern provinces such as Holland and Zeeland. Their growing resentment at Spanish rule, especially after King Philip of Spain sent the brutal duke of Alva to quell anti-Spanish activity and enforce Counter-Reformation doctrine, eventually provoked outright revolt. In 1579 five provinces united to declare their independence of Spain, and a republic was born which was to become one of the greatest trading powers in seventeenth-century Europe.

King Philip managed to hold the southern provinces but the United (Dutch) Provinces struggled to retain their newly won independence and, under the leadership of William of Orange, they sought assistance from abroad. He appealed to Elizabeth for men and money, emphasising their common Protestant identities. This put Elizabeth in a dilemma. On the one hand, she had no sympathy for anyone rebelling against a lawfully constituted monarch and she was not inclined to expend the necessary sums on another country's behalf. On the other hand, William of Orange was also soliciting the help of the duke of Anjou, brother of the king of France, and Elizabeth did not want a potentially hostile Franco-Dutch alliance across the channel. Reluctantly she allowed herself to be drawn into the conflict and in 1585 provided troops and money. It was to be an enormous drain on English resources – at a time when England was also supporting Henri of Navarre with men and money, as well as maintaining a large army in Ireland.

In the end the Netherlands were never reunited. The United (Protestant) Provinces went their own way while the remaining southern provinces remained under Catholic Habsburg rule, eventually emerging as modern-day Belgium. As well as being religiously different, the two territories also had quite distinct cultural identities: the south retained the civilised veneer imposed by the Habsburg court, with its sombre beauty and magnificent artistic achievements, while the north, under Calvinist iconoclastic influence, was inclined towards austerity and simplicity. Thus the contrast between the Papists and the Puritan Protestants at the end of the sixteenth century was neatly demonstrated in the Netherlands.

Conclusion

At the end of the sixteenth century the Netherlands were accommodating Catholics and Puritan Protestants. Spain, on the other hand, was unequivocally committed to Catholicism, which was rigorously upheld by the Inquisition. France, too, remained a Catholic country though, for the time being at least, it was prepared to tolerate its Protestant population. By the end of Elizabeth's reign the Irish Catholics had been subdued. She was succeeded by James VI of Scotland, who had long experience of managing conflict between Papists and Presbyterian Protestants.

Document case study

2.1 Calvin's view of the Godly Magistrates

From The institutes of the Christian Religion, *Calvin's interpretation of Christian doctrine*

Godly Magistrates
The Lord has not only testified that the office of magistrate is approved and acceptable to him, but he also sets out its dignity with the most honourable titles and marvellously commends it to us . . . They have a mandate from God, having been invested with divine authority, and are wholly God's representatives acting as what might be called his viceregents. This is no subtlety of mine, but Christ's explanation. 'If scripture', he says, 'called them gods to whom the word of God came . . .' (John 10, 35) . . . Accordingly there should be no doubt that civil authority is a calling, not only holy and lawful before God, but also the most sacred and by far the most honourable of all callings in the whole life of mortal men . . .

This consideration ought continually to occupy the magistrates themselves, since it can greatly spur them to exercise their office and bring them notable comfort to mitigate their tasks, which are indeed many and burdensome. For what great zeal for uprightness, prudence, greatness, self-control and innocence ought to be required of those who know that their judgement seat is like the throne of the living God?

Obedience to just and unjust magistrates
Let no one be deceived here. Since the magistrate cannot be resisted without God resisted at the same time . . .

Source: John Calvin, *The institutes of the Christian religion* (1534–59), IV, xx, 4, 6, 23, in G. R. Potter and M. Greengrass (eds.), John Calvin, London, 1983, pp. 60–61, 63

2.2 A Puritan's opinion of princely authority

From the writings of an English Protestant in exile during the reign of Mary Tudor

. . . Princes therefore, and all powers upon the earth, are not to be compared unto God, whose Lieutenants only they should be, and are no longer than he will, in whose hands their hearts are, to move and turn at his pleasure. And for that cause it is their duty to seek all means possible, whereby the glory of God might be advanced, by whom they are themselves so highly exalted above their brethren, and in no cause to minister occasion of rebellion against his mighty Majesty: but rather to be examples to others (over whom they are constitute) of all Godly life and lawful obedience . . .

Source: Christopher Goodman, *How superior powers ought to be obeyed by their subjects* . . ., Geneva, 1558, in Edmund S. Morgan (ed.), *Puritan political ideas 1558–1794*, Indianapolis, 1965, pp. 4–5

2.3 The role of the secular ruler according to the Scottish parliament

From The Confession of Faith, ratified by the Scottish parliament on 17 August 1560

The Confession of Faith professed and believed by the Protestants within the Realm of Scotland published by them in parliament and by the estates thereof ratified and approved as wholesome and sound doctrine grounded upon the infallible truth of God's word.

[There follow 23 headings, including:]
Of the Civil Magistrate
We confess and acknowledge empires, kingdoms, dominions and cities to be distinguished and ordained by God . . . for manifestation of his own glory and for the singular profit and commodity of mankind so that whosoever goes about to take away or to confound the whole state of civil policies now long established we affirm the same men not only to be enemies to mankind but also wickedly to fight against God's expressed will.

. . . Moreover to kings, princes, rulers and magistrates we affirm that chiefly and most principally the conservation and remedy of the religion appertains so that not only they are appointed for civil policy but also for maintenance of the true religion and for suppressing of idolatry and superstition . . .

Source: *The Acts of the parliament of Scotland*, Thomas Thomson and Cosmo Nelson Innes (eds.), 10 vols., London, 1814–75, vol. II, pp. 526, 533–34 [translated and modernised by the author]

2.4 Confirming the spiritual and temporal authority of Queen Elizabeth I

From the Act of Supremacy, 1559

IX. And for the better observation and maintenance of this Act . . . every archbishop, bishop, and . . . other ecclesiastical person . . . and every other person having your Highness' fee or wages . . . shall make, take and receive a corporal oath upon the Evangelist . . . to the tenor and effect hereafter following, that is to say:

I, A. B., do utterly testify and declare in my conscience, that the Queen's Highness is the only Supreme Governor of this realm and all other her Highness' dominions and countries, as well in all spiritual and ecclesiastical things or causes as temporal, and that no foreign prince, person, prelate state or potentate hath or ought to have any jurisdiction, power, superiority, pre-eminence or authority, ecclesiastical or spiritual within this realm; and therefore I do utterly renounce and forsake all foreign juris-dictions, powers, superiorities and authorities, and do promise that from henceforth I shall bear faith and true allegiance to the Queen's Highness, her heirs and lawful successors, and to my power shall assist and defend all jurisdictions, pre-eminences, privileges and authorities granted or belonging to the Queen's Highness, her heirs and successors, or united or annexed to the imperial crown of this realm: so help me God, and by the contents of this Book.

Source: G. W. Prothero (ed.), *Select statutes and other constitutional documents illustrative of the reigns of Elizabeth and James I*, Oxford, 1894, pp. 6–7

Document case-study questions

The questions are based on the documents but you may need to look elsewhere in the book for relevant information.

1 What views does Calvin express in 2.1 regarding secular authority?

2 How were Calvin's views modified by those who found themselves in opposition to secular authority (2.2)?

3 What were the responsibilities of rulers as interpreted by the Scottish parliament (2.3)?

4 Explain the chief obligations of royal servants according to the oath imposed upon them by the English parliament (2.4)?

5 Compare the Scottish parliament's interpretation of the role of the secular ruler in ecclesiastical matters (2.3) with that of the English parliament (2.4).

3 The Jacobean church

When James VI of Scotland rode south in 1603 to become James I of England, and Supreme Governor of the English church, hopes were raised in the hearts of those from right across the religious spectrum. Consequently, the religious context of the early years of James I's reign can best be seen in terms of the rival claims of expectant Catholics and Puritans. The Catholics were convinced that the son of Mary, queen of Scots, martyred for her Roman Catholic faith, would declare his allegiance to Rome. The Puritans were equally sure that one who had been brought up in Presbyterian Scotland would be in tune with their desire to further reform the church. He was subject to appeals from representatives from both Catholics and Puritans for an improvement in their fortunes, almost immediately.

James's religious outlook

It is difficult precisely to identify James's religious position. This was probably because James took such care to avoid revealing it. He was a keen theologian with a genuinely open mind who delighted in reasoned argument and was willing to listen to any intelligently expressed opinion. His view of the Roman Catholic Church was that it was mistaken rather than fundamentally flawed. He wrote: 'I reverence their church as our mother church, although clogged with many infirmities and corruptions.' He did not object to Catholics because of their beliefs – it was the pope's claim to depose a monarch and release his subjects from allegiance to their king which underlay James's opposition to Catholicism. In other words, it was the question of authority, rather than theology, which was at the centre of his objection to the Catholics. Furthermore, one of his greatest strengths in his later years as king of Scotland had been his ability to manage opposing groups or factions, including religious factions. James recognised that control and not elimination of any group was the more desirable course. He saw only the most radical elements of both religious wings as a threat to the stability of the church and state. Thus he sought to incorporate the moderates into the Jacobean church in England, a policy which had served him well in Scotland.

Although James's education had been staunchly Calvinist, at the hands of the scholarly and devout George Buchanan, he tended towards the less extreme expression of the doctrine. For instance, he was patently opposed to the wholesale reorganisation of ecclesiastical government on the Presbyterian model favoured by the kirk in Scotland. This model divided the religious from the

concessions to them to smooth the peace he made with Spain, bringing the Spanish wars to an end in 1604. Although he soon allayed some of the Protestants' doubts by issuing proclamations and passing laws against the Catholics, they were not completely reassured and continued to press James to make his intentions more clear.

James, however, was striving to detach the moderate Catholics from the more uncompromising element. He had declared that he did not intend to persecute anyone for reason of conscience, a policy he had adopted in Scotland. The majority of English Catholics were only too willing to keep their heads down, remaining loyal to the crown but quietly adhering to the practices of the old church. Unfortunately, his efforts were jeopardised by the Puritans, who saw any relaxation towards the Catholics as an overture to a complete toleration. When James cautioned the godly magistrates to modify their severe implementation of the recent laws against the Catholics – which had prompted the Catholics to engage in their own petitioning campaign to the king – they obstinately interpreted it as a direct threat to their own position. The king was dismayed to discover that his attitude towards the Catholics had been misconstrued by his new subjects, and there were rumours that he meant to allow them toleration to practise their faith. Accordingly, he passionately declared his hostility to the Roman Catholic Church and, as part of the tightening up of local administration, he demanded renewed activity against Catholic recusants. This provoked a small number of Catholics to involve themselves in the notorious Gunpowder Plot, contrary to the explicit orders of the pope. The plot is one of the enduring mysteries of history, prompting endless debate about the circumstances surrounding it. Its consequence was further anti-Catholic legislation in the parliament of 1606 – including the introduction of an Oath of Allegiance (to the king). However, this legislation was aimed at only those Catholics who refused to acknowledge their loyalty to the crown and who refused to pay their recusancy fines. This reflected James's attitude towards Catholics – he regarded them as a political, and not a religious, problem. Indeed, recent historians have pointed out that although James did not grant the Catholic community formal toleration, he did offer moderate and loyal Catholics tolerance. In other words, the practice of Roman Catholicism was passively ignored rather than actively allowed.

Religion in Scotland and Ireland

The early seventeenth-century church, then, was capable of incorporating a wide range of religious opinion. There is little doubt that the force which contained these differences was King James himself. He was dedicated to unity rather than uniformity; he demanded minimal conformity; and he recognised the political advantage in not alienating particular groups. Yet, if the English church benefited from the personal attention of its king, how would the Scottish kirk fare in his absence? At first there seemed to be little problem. He had promised to return to Scotland every three years, when he could keep a supervisory eye on its progress.

In the event he made just one visit to Scotland, in 1617. By then the Scottish kirk had become accustomed to running its own affairs. Given the lack of conflict in Scottish religion, James was willing to countenance this, with a few exceptions. He insisted on the reintroduction of bishops to Scotland and, in 1618, he forced upon the kirk a number of liturgical reforms (i.e. changes in the form of church service). Known as the Five Articles of Perth, they were deeply unpopular, and James (probably wisely, given what happened twenty years later – see below, pp. 42–43) refrained from further interference.

James dealt with Ireland in much the same way. Elizabeth's efforts in Ireland were a grim example of the consequences of punitive anti-Catholic measures. When the two most powerful Catholic earls fled to Europe in 1607 – an event known as the 'flight of the earls' – it marked a suspension of Irish resistance to English rule. Their extensive lands were confiscated and given to Calvinist Scots and English settlers, a process which developed into the plantation (i.e. colonisation) of Ulster. Although this might have been an opportunity to impose religious uniformity on the Irish, James, prudently, declined to take it. Even the Calvinist nature of the Irish Articles (of religion) adopted by Convocation in 1615 did not present any real problems. Thus, in his 'three kingdoms' James avoided making religion a major divisive issue.

Continental influences on English religion

The strength of the English church under the government of James was its ability to embrace the diverse and competitive threads of English Protestantism. As well as the king's interest and influence, though, there was another factor which helped James achieve his ambition of a broad-based church. This was the value of England at peace with her European neighbours. Whenever Continental considerations got in the way, any harmony within the church became more fragile. As part of his balanced approach, James resolved to marry his eldest son to a Catholic and his daughter to a Protestant. In 1613 he married his daughter, Elizabeth, to the ultra-Protestant Frederick V of the Palatinate (one of several states in the Holy Roman Empire which was located in the area of modern-day Germany). To maintain a balance, James sought a Catholic princess for his heir, Henry. The most serious proposal was for a match with the Infanta (princess) of Spain. Naturally, this raised alarm and suspicion in the hearts of the more extreme Calvinists, who were concerned that the marriage settlement would improve conditions for English Catholics. There was sustained Puritan agitation over the Spanish match (now with Charles, after the death of Henry in 1612) and this continued into the 1620s. Then, in 1618, there was a development which polarised religious opinion in England: the outbreak of the Thirty Years War in central Europe.

Contrary to his father-in-law's advice, in 1619 Frederick had accepted the throne of Bohemia (another state in the Holy Roman Empire). It was vacant as a result of a Protestant revolt against their Bohemian king, the Catholic Ferdinand. When the deposed King Ferdinand was elected Holy Roman Emperor in the same year, he was in a position to retaliate. The dispute escalated into a major conflict between the Catholic and Protestant powers of central Europe which was to last for the next thirty years. In 1620 Frederick was ousted from Bohemia, as well as from the Palatinate, and James was forced to become involved on behalf of his daughter and son-in-law. His Protestant subjects expected him to become the champion of European Protestantism and instigate a military campaign to recover the Palatinate. James, on the other hand, was determined to effect its recovery by diplomatic means. Central to his policy were continuing negotiations for a Spanish match. If Spain were an ally, the Spanish king might be persuaded to bring his influence to bear over his Habsburg cousin in central Europe to restore the Palatinate to Frederick. Moreover, James was determined not to become involved in a war of religion.

For a proportion of James's population, however, an alliance with Catholic Spain (and by extension with the Holy Roman Emperor) against Protestant Europe was anathema. They were horrified at the prospect and urged him to take up arms to recover the Palatinate. The most vociferous among them were the Puritans and moderate Calvinists, many of whom sat in James's parliament. But, while they pressed for war, they were less keen to vote him the necessary money to pay for it. It has been argued that the perverseness displayed by the godly in parliament, who were demanding war but refusing to finance it, while at the same time opposing James's efforts to follow a diplomatic policy, drove James into the arms of the Arminians (see below).

The Arminian challenge to the Jacobean church

Certainly, the outbreak of the Thirty Years War challenged the consensus which James had achieved in the English church, when he had successfully detached the moderate from the more extreme elements. In his pursuit of a broad-based church, James had sought to appoint bishops of all shades of Protestantism, thus creating a balanced episcopal bench. He aimed at an episcopate which reflected all but the most extreme elements of his population. Accordingly, his bishops were recruited from among highly committed Calvinists such as George Abbot, John King, James Montagu and Arthur Lake. He also elevated a number of so-called Arminians, such as Richard Neile, Lancelot Andrewes, John Buckridge and Gilbert Overall. The Arminians were a small group who subscribed to the teachings of the Dutch theologian Jacob Arminius. They questioned Calvinist doctrines, in particular the Calvinist teaching on predestination. Instead of the rigid interpretation adopted by the more zealous Calvinists, they believed that divine grace was freely available and they allowed for the possibility that human will enabled people to shape their own destiny. They were also committed to reintroducing into the church some of the elements of beauty which had been abandoned by the Calvinists.

In the reign of James, Arminianism was relatively uncontentious. However, when it was adopted by King Charles I, after the death of James, it began to be viewed with increased suspicion. It was identified with radicalism and even

Roman Catholicism, and its opponents used 'Arminian' as a pejorative term – in much the same way as 'Puritan' had been. Consequently, many historians prefer to use a more neutral term, such as 'Laudian' (identified with William Laud, archbishop of Canterbury) or 'ceremonialist'.

Once again, it is difficult to gauge how far James subscribed to Arminianism but it is unlikely that he was subject to undue influence by Arminians. Certainly, their lack of fanaticism will have appealed to him, but his inclusion of Arminians onto the episcopal bench was more an expression of his traditional desire to achieve balance – within his church as well as elsewhere – rather than an indication he had fallen for the Arminian view. James's episcopate was of a remarkably high quality. They worked diligently in their dioceses and strived to improve standards amongst the parish clergy. They also ensured that the interests of the church were represented at the centre. Paradoxically, these were the very same ambitions held by the more radical Puritans.

As Puritanism became identified with aggressively anti-Catholic and anti-Spanish attitudes, Puritans were looking increasingly like the kind of dissident and potentially dangerous faction they had seemed at the beginning of the reign. Thus it was reasonable that their anti-Calvinist or Arminian opponents might seem more attractive to the king. But although James, in his usual open-minded way, was prepared to listen to Arminian arguments, there is no evidence that he was overly influenced by what he heard. For example, his suspicion of Arminians as heterodox (i.e. contrary to orthodox or accepted opinion) and factional agitators was illustrated in 1618 by his directions to the English delegates to the Synod of Dort (a conference held to consider how best to deal with the Arminians in the Low Countries) to support the anti-Arminian majority. Although he later modified his sentiments regarding Arminianism, he never wholly revised them.

Matters hotted up in 1624, when Richard Montagu published his notorious work *A new gag for an old goose*, a defence of the established Protestant church in which he rejected the Calvinist doctrine of predestination. It caused a furore and outraged the Calvinist clergy. *The new gag* had been written in response to a Catholic tract called *A gag for the new gospel*, which asserted that the Protestant church in England was essentially Calvinist or Puritan. This, according to Montagu, was wholly erroneous. In order to demonstrate that the English church was neither Papist nor Puritan, nor a satellite of either Rome or Geneva, he produced this definition of the Anglican Church, which he hoped would 'stand in the gap between puritanism and popery' by playing down the points of difference between the Roman Catholic Church and the Church of England.

To many low churchmen Montagu's views appeared to be heresy, and he was denounced in the 1624 parliament as dangerously inclined towards Arminianism and a threat to the established church. James ordered him to review and reform his book. However, when he came to re-examine his book Montagu found that, rather than inclining towards a more moderate position, he felt more strongly than ever about the dangerous and subversive Calvinist influence over the Anglican Church. He therefore produced another work – the *Appello Caesarem* – which was an even more forceful exposition of his views. At this point James died and, when the church was more volatile than it had been for years, its supervision was in the hands of Charles I.

Conclusion

The broad-based church achieved by James was one of the principal achievements of his reign. Although it received a slight set-back with the outbreak of the Thirty Years War it nevertheless survived intact into Charles I's reign. Both Catholic and Puritan moderates had been accommodated into the English church. James was managing Arminian and Calvinist pressure groups with considerable skill. Despite his policy towards the Puritans being undermined in the last years of his reign, moderate and conforming Calvinists continued to enjoy relative freedom of activity at the parish level. At the same time, the Catholics benefited from James's more relaxed approach. Unfortunately, his successor was not of sufficient calibre to be entrusted with the Jacobean consensus.

Document case study

3.1 A Catholic petition to King James I for a conference with the Protestants

From A Petition Apologetical, presented to the King's most Excellent Majesty, by the Lay Catholics of England, dated 24 September 1604

Reasons of publishing this treatise

The publishing of this apology cannot but tend much to his Majesty's honour, and more to his satisfaction and security; for so much as the Catholics' affectionate services and obligations therein contained, must needs be arguments of some supereminent virtue and goodness in his sacred personage, that could draw from them at all times such extraordinary effects of love and devotion: and the more manifest the protestations of their purgations* shall appear to the world, the more manifold shall be their bonds and obligations of performance, and perseverance therein.

The Protestant prelates cannot with reason disallow thereof, because herein is nothing required at their hands, but a reasonable conference, and satisfaction in points of their mission and vocation: and when they shall make it evident out of the written word, that they are the true shepherds and pastors sent from God to have charge of souls, they make proffer without delay to follow them, and with all conformity to obey them, and hear their voices; which when they shall prove, the controversy is charitably composed, and though they fail of their proofs, yet they remain, as they do with their wealth, their wives, their pleasures, and palaces: the poore Catholics desiring only a secret and silent permission of such pastors, as shall show to them and the whole world, sufficient evidence and approbation for the charge of souls they undertake.

The Puritans herewith cannot be offended, if they peaceably, and precisely seek after contentment, and not contention: because they shall find divers of their maxims zealously, or rather odiously conceived by them against Catholics, overthrown and evacuated by most evident demonstration and instances in matters of fact, practice, and experience: especially in that point of conditional subjects, which is so much urged by the ministry.

---

* the taking of an oath to cleanse oneself from accusation or suspicion

Source: A. W. Pollard and G. R. Redgrave (eds.), *A short title catalogue of books printed in England, Scotland and Ireland* (2nd edn), no. 4835 [spelling modernised by the author]

3.2 A Puritan petition to King James on behalf of their ministers faced with losing their livings

From The Humble Petition of your Majesty's Loyal and True-hearted Subjects, Justices of Peace and Gentlemen within your Highness's County of Northampton, presented 9 February 1605

To the King's most Excellent Majesty. [We] most humbly beg and crave of your Highness that the hand of your kingly favour may be stretched out to moderate the extremity of this decree which otherwise is like to deprive us, and thousands of your loyal and true-hearted people, of the labours of many faithful preachers who not out of a will and conceitedness (as some have supposed), but out of the tenderness of their consciences, and fear to offend the King of Heaven (as we are verily persuaded), make scruple to use the ceremonies, and yield to the subscription enjoined. We presume, most dread sovereign (out of our love of the truth of God) and out of our loyal hearts to your Majesty with confident boldness to affirm in your princely presence that these men, for whom we sue, have laboured long amongst us; with great pains and faithfulness profited us and many of your subjects by their conscionable* and sincere teaching; confuted Papism; repressed Brownism; and all other schismatical and heretical opinions carefully; beaten down sin and impiety powerfully, and have proved lights of great comfort and furtherance to us and all others your Majesty's subjects within their several charges, both by their doctrine and examples.

. . . So shall your Majesty glorify the God of heaven; honour your royal person; maintain the laws of your kingdom; proceed in the gracious way of her Majesty deceased; be a means of the salvation of the souls of many [of] your subjects; encourage many young students to the study of divinity; take away this unnecessary occasion of contention in the church; keep your Majesty's subjects from schism and separation; daunt the hearts of Papists and atheists who glory much in the deprivation of painful** pastors and teachers; raise up the spirits of your sorrowful people; and bind us all, as in duty we are most bound, to pray daily and hourly for the preservation of your person, the prosperity of your government and the prolonging of your days; and that there may never want one from your kingly loins to sit on your throne.

---

* conscientious
** diligent

Source: Public Record Office, State Papers 14/12/69i, printed in Claire Cross (ed.), *The letters of Sir Francis Hastings*, Somerset Record Society (vol. 69, 1969), pp. 88–89 [spelling modernised by the author]

Document case-study questions

The questions are based on the documents but you may need to look elsewhere in the book for relevant information.

1 What are the Catholics hoping for from the new king (3.1)?
2 How realistic are their expectations (3.1)?
3 Discuss the concerns of the Puritans expressed in 3.2 regarding the imminent loss of many of their ministers?
4 Comment on the petitioners' warnings in 3.2 if they are not heeded?
5 How do the two petitions in 3.1 and 3.2 illustrate the different interests of the Catholics and the Puritans at the beginning of James I's English reign?

4 The Caroline church

James I was succeeded by his son, Charles. The failure of the male line of the house of Tudor meant that the sixteenth century had been dominated by a series of succession crises and it had been well over a century since an undisputed, healthy, adult male had ascended the English throne. But the situation in 1625 was very different from that in 1509: at that time the country was united in religious terms, and the accession of Henry VIII effectively brought to an end the civil strife which had raged between the rival houses of York and Lancaster. Now, in Scotland, Ireland and Wales, as well as in England, there were Papists, Protestants and varieties of Puritans, with the added complication of a growing 'Arminian' element.

James had managed to achieve a broad-based English church which embraced all but those holding the most radical religious views. Charles, though, was temperamentally unsuited to maintaining his father's balanced church. He has been described as a man of tunnel vision, with room apparently for only one point of view, and it looked as if he might succumb to the increasingly authoritarian and absolutist attractions of Arminianism. Furthermore, while James had deliberately played down the religious aspect of the escalating conflict on the Continent, Charles was only too willing to become involved as the champion of Protestantism.

Arminianism versus Puritanism

The religious situation inherited by Charles I was one of consensus within a largely united Protestant church. Only the more extreme, 'hotter sort' of Protestants – or Puritans – were regarded as any kind of threat to the general accord. They were seen as a small, albeit menacing, minority. The majority were perfectly comfortable with conventional forms of church service and the easy-going Prayer Book; they completely rejected Puritan demands for Presbyterianism while they fully endorsed the office of bishop within the church. Arminianism, therefore, appeared to reflect their views more closely. Even the most radical Arminian precept which questioned predestination was greeted by many with a measure of relief.

The new king displayed a decisive bias towards Arminianism, exemplified by his appointment of Richard Montagu as a royal chaplain in 1625. The following February Charles ordered a theological debate to take place at York House (the London residence of his favourite, George Villiers, duke of Buckingham) in front of an audience composed of representatives from all shades of religious opinion. Its purpose was to discuss Montagu's writing – which had been fiercely criticised in the previous reign (see above, p. 33) – and Arminianism in general. In the event, it boiled down to a polemic between the Arminian bishop Buckridge and the Calvinist bishop Morton about how the doctrine of predestination could be reconciled with the Prayer Book teaching regarding baptism and communion. Although the York House Conference did not reach any formal conclusions, it became clear from its proceedings that Buckingham – who always reflected the king's position – was inclined towards Arminianism. 'Predestination theology', the central plank of Calvinist doctrine, was comprehensively rejected while 'predestination' was defined as 'a kind of heresy' in the standard Latin dictionary.

Charles's choice of William Laud to preach at the opening of the 1625 and 1626 parliaments, and to supervise his coronation service, was a further indication of the king's religious inclination. In 1621 King James had wearily submitted to demands from Charles and Buckingham to elevate the pro-Arminian and anti-Calvinist Laud to the bishopric of St David's, adding a warning about the outcome of promoting him. Charles and Buckingham, however, continued to endorse Laud, especially after Charles became king. It used to be thought that Laud exerted considerable influence over Charles and was responsible for shaping his religious views, but recent historians are inclined to believe that Laud was simply reflecting his master's wishes. The most recent study (Julian Davies, *The Caroline captivity of the church*) traces the innovations of the 1630s – such as increased ceremonialism – to Charles rather than to the rise of Arminianism. It would seem that throughout his reign Charles was personally responsible for the direction of the English church, which, very soon after James's death, shifted distinctly away from Calvinism.

Later in 1626 Buckingham became the chancellor of Cambridge University, where there was a strong Puritan presence. Nevertheless, Calvinist teaching was declared illegal and dangerous and, soon after, a royal proclamation virtually outlawed Calvinist doctrine. But whereas the London and Cambridge printing presses caved in to the ban on Calvinist material immediately, Oxford, where the Calvinist earl of Pembroke was chancellor, held out for another two years. In the meantime Charles had the Thirty-Nine Articles, on which the whole of the established English church rested, reissued, together with a preface declaring the literal and grammatical sense of them, thereby putting an end to all speculation.

Reaction in parliament was strident. Many members of the House of Commons were Puritans and they retaliated to the developments in the church by declaring Arminianism to be heterodox (i.e. contrary to accepted opinion). Arminianism was even seen as a means of introducing Roman Catholicism into England through the back door, given the apparent ceremonial similarities between the two. Throughout the parliaments of 1624 to 1629, the House of Commons, led by John Pym, vigorously attacked the rise of Arminianism. In 1629, during Charles's last parliament for 11 years, the Commons resolved to 'avow for truth . . . that sense of the Articles of Religion' as defined by 'the public acts of the Church of

England and by the general and current expositions of the writers of our Church'. In other words, they were determined to defend the English church which had been settled by Convocation and confirmed by statute (i.e. by parliament).

That they felt it was under threat was demonstrated when they went on to reject 'the sense [i.e. the interpretation of religion] of the Jesuits, Arminians, and all others who differ from it'. As a final desperate measure, the first of the Three Protestations of the Commons, which were read while the Speaker was held down in his chair (to ensure the continuation of the parliamentary session), concerned Arminianism. It declared that 'Whoever shall bring in innovation of religion, or by favour or countenance seek to extend or introduce popery or Arminianism, or other opinion disagreeing from the true and orthodox Church, shall be reputed a capital enemy to this kingdom and Commonwealth.' There was little doubt what Arminianism stood for in the eyes of the Calvinist or Puritan members of parliament.

Charles's decision to rule without reference to parliament – the Eleven Years' Personal Rule (1629–40) – left the Puritans with no institution to challenge the crown's interpretation of disputed issues of either a religious or a secular nature. The Personal Rule began by tackling one of the fundamental issues which separated Calvinist and Arminian thinking. This concerned the placing of the communion table in the parish church. The propensity of the Arminians to refer to it as the 'altar', with all its popish connotations, together with their insistence on placing it at one end of the church, and railed off, deeply offended the Calvinists. It also appeared directly to transgress the Elizabethan injunction which decreed that it should be moved into the main body of the church during the eucharist. Many parishioners were already outraged by Arminian variations of church services. When uniformity of church service was imposed, in the 1630s, which meant the Arminian practice regarding the communion table had to be comprehensively adopted, it provoked widespread opposition.

Resolving the altar controversy was only the first of a series of measures taken by Laud – who had become archbishop of Canterbury in 1633 – and his fellow Arminians. In the face of a decline in ecclesiastical discipline, which Laud felt was undermining the position of the church, he determined to restore the authority and standing of the clergy in the parishes. He also effected a corresponding promotion of the episcopate (bishops) by emphasising their position as God's lieutenants on earth. In turn, this developed into the theory of the divine right of bishops and its complementary notion of the divine right of kings (i.e. that bishops and kings derived their authority from God and not from subordinates or subjects). At the same time, increasing numbers of parish priests were appointed onto the commissions of the peace (as JPs) and there was a much stronger presence of churchmen in the privy council. On the face of it, this active participation in the government of the realm at every level was precisely what the Puritans wished for; but it was Arminian clergy and bishops, not Puritans, who achieved these positions of influence.

Perhaps inevitably, the Puritans grew increasingly hostile towards the bishops, who seemed to epitomise the kind of regime which Laud (as Charles's agent) was imposing upon England. Initially, the anti-episcopal movement was confined to the lower orders of society, but gradually the gentry began to adopt similar sentiments, and criticism of the episcopate became more vociferous. In 1637, three distinguished Puritan leaders – John Bastwick, Henry Burton and William Prynne – were sentenced to stand in the pillory and have their ears cropped (Prynne's ears had already been cut off in 1634) before ending their days in

THE FIRST ACT.

Enter the Bishop of Canterbury, and with him a Doctor of Physicke, a Lawyer, and a Divine ; who being set downe, they bring him variety of Dishes to his Table,

C *Anterbury,* is here all the dishes, that are provided?
   Doct. My Lord, there is all : and 'tis enough, wert for a Princes table, Ther's **24.** severall dainty dishes, and all rare.
   B, *Cant.* Are these rare : no, no, they please me not,
Give me a Carbinadoed cheek, or a tippet of a Cocks combe .
None of all this, here is meate for my Pallet.
   Lawyer. My Lord, here is both Cocke and Phesant,
Quaile and **Partridge,** and the best varieties the shambles yeeld.

A Puritan satire on archbishop Laud dining off the ears of William Prynne (cut off as a punishment for writing pamphlets condemning stage plays). What conclusions can be drawn about Puritan anxiety regarding the state's attitudes to their brethren?

prison. Their crime had been to publish anti-episcopal pamphlets. They were hailed as heroes and attracted enormous popular support as victims of Laudianism, which was identified with repression and innovation.

Laud's own position had been confirmed when the Calvinist archbishop of Canterbury, George Abbot, died in 1633. Abbot, who represented an alternative position to that adopted by the king, had been increasingly marginalised as an authority within the church. He was succeeded by Laud and, together, the king and his new archbishop of Canterbury extended their efforts to promote order and decency in church services while restoring much of the beauty and holiness which had been lost since the Reformation. One of the chief attractions of the Arminians, to Charles, was the way in which they expressed the majesty of kingship through restrained but exquisite glorification. As Arminianism was adopted as a legitimising agent in support of the power and authority of the sovereign it began to be associated with both neo-absolutism and crypto-Catholicism – in other words, arbitrary government and popery. It was also identified by many of the gentry with a dissolute and idle 'court' as opposed to a pure and hardworking 'country'.

Certainly, the court was becoming increasingly isolated from Calvinist opinion in the country. In 1618, recognising that working men needed an opportunity to refresh their spirits, King James I had issued the *Book of Sports*, which defined those activities permitted on Sundays. This was despite the demands of the godly (Puritan) magistrates in the regions that such activities be drastically curtailed. They felt that their endeavours to maintain discipline in their unruly communities were seriously undermined by official sanctioning of 'dancing and leaping and vaulting'. Charles's decision to reissue the *Book of Sports* in 1633 caused enormous resentment for he too seemed to be abrogating his duty to uphold law and order. When Laud intervened to promote the holding of 'wakes' (similar to church fêtes) in Somerset, contrary to the wishes of the county magistrates, he appeared to be confirming the view that central government had scant regard for the rule of law.

The position of the Catholics

The late sixteenth and early seventeenth centuries were punctuated by fears that popery would triumph over Protestantism. The Spanish Armada in 1588, the Gunpowder Plot in 1605, the consequences of the Spanish match in the later years of James I's reign, and invasion scares when England was at war with the two great Catholic powers – France and Spain – in the 1620s, were rounded off with rumours of a popish plot in the late 1630s. But how rational were these fears and why did they climax in the reign of Charles I? The two obvious factors were, firstly, that Charles's queen was a Catholic who openly practised her religion and appeared to have encouraged the conversion of some highly placed courtiers and members of the government to Catholicism. The second concerned the disturbing similarities between the ceremonial and language of Arminianism and Roman Catholicism.

The situation was complicated by Charles's decision to rule without parliament, which meant that he was obliged to seek financial support from quarters other than traditional parliamentary levies. One alternative source of revenue was the English Catholic community, who continued to be subject to hefty recusancy fines. But Charles was faced with a dilemma, for over-rigorous enforcement of recusancy penalties would impoverish a useful source of continuous monetary supply. Therefore it made sense to relax *somewhat* the burden placed upon Catholics and, accordingly, Charles proposed a scheme whereby they could lease back confiscated lands, thereby injecting more money into the exchequer. Unfortunately, despite denials from the king, such moves were interpreted as a lack of constancy against popery and were deeply unpopular. In fact, penal laws against Catholics were so effectively enforced under Charles that a clear divide opened up between those Catholics living in the country, who were subject to tough financial burdens, and Catholics at court, who appeared to enjoy a privileged existence.

Despite this dichotomy, anti-Catholic feelings continued to make an impact on English society. They were sharpened when Charles was in conflict with the more radical Protestants in Scotland and sought Catholic support, both at home and abroad, against them. By the time Charles recalled parliament in 1640, religious tension had reached such a pitch that rumours of a popish plot were receiving widespread credibility. Although there never was a plot, it was a measure of the atmosphere of hysteria that the popular imagination feared one. Matters were not helped by Charles's unwillingness, or inability, to explain himself. Even so, it was not the king who was the principal target of parliament's retaliation to perceived Catholic pretensions, but his advisers. And when parliament raised its army in the summer of 1642, it was in defence of the king and the preservation of the Protestant religion.

Scotland

James's dealings with the Scottish kirk had been cautious. Laud, however, who had been with James on his one visit to Scotland after his accession to the English throne, could see no merit in his circumspection. He felt that not enough had been done to reconcile the Scottish kirk with the English church. Under Charles, Laud was able to proceed more rigorously in the religious affairs of Scotland. When Laud accompanied Charles to Scotland in 1633, they both were shocked by the sparse Scottish kirks and were determined to impose on Scotland a model more like the Anglican Church which they were developing in England. Laud worked closely with his Scottish brethren in drawing up a new Prayer Book, which was ready in 1637. Its imposition on Scotland by royal prerogative, without reference to the General Assembly (of representatives of the kirk), marked the peak of the campaign for uniformity. It appeared to epitomise arbitrary rule from London. When the inevitable rioting against the use of the Prayer Book erupted, the remarkable spectacle of the bishop of Brechin reading the Prayer Book over loaded pistols pointed at his congregation, was testimony to the way in which the situation was rapidly getting beyond control.

Resistance mounted. Following a petition drawn up in October 1637, which condemned the Prayer Book for its encouragement of idolatry and false doctrine, thousands of Scotsmen subscribed to the National Covenant of 1638. This bound the signatories, or Covenanters, to maintain the true faith, as embodied by the Kirk of Scotland, in the face of 'innovations and evils which have no warrant in the Word of God'. Support for the Covenant, though by no means unanimous, made it a formidable movement and the Covenanters took the opportunity to demand the recall of the Scottish parliament and the General Assembly. When the General Assembly met, in 1638, bishops were abolished.

Charles, faced with rebellion in Scotland, was determined to suppress it. An English army marched north in the summer of 1639 to deal with the forces raised by the leading Covenanters, such as the earl of Argyll. The confrontation – which came to be known as the First Bishops' War – was an inconclusive affair, and a peace of sorts was arranged. Sweeping concessions were demanded of Charles, which were to lead to the introduction of an extreme Presbyterian Scottish church. How far Charles felt bound by these concessions can only be a matter of speculation, but the general consensus among historians is that he had no intention of honouring them for any longer than he had to.

Ireland

Although Irish Protestants comprised only a fraction of the population of Ireland, they held a considerable proportion of the land. The established Church of Ireland represented their position. It was largely Presbyterian or Calvinist in outlook, which was reflected in the Irish Articles adopted by the Convocation of 1615. In many respects the Irish church was more firmly Calvinist than its English counterpart had ever been, probably because it had to make its presence felt alongside a large Catholic majority who continued to practise their religion free from interference. When Charles and Laud turned their attention to Irish religious affairs in the 1630s, therefore, they found a church in need of rescue from excessive Calvinist influence. With the enthusiastic support of the new Lord Deputy of Ireland, Thomas Wentworth (appointed in 1632), Laud began bringing the Church of Ireland closer to the church which was being constructed in England. A recent examination of this period concludes that Laud and Wentworth interfered in an unprecedented way in the affairs of the Irish church, beginning with a Convocation in 1634 which accepted Charles's anti-Calvinist interpretation of the Thirty-Nine Articles. A Court of High Commission, designed to deal with recalcitrant Puritan ministers, crushed further Calvinist opposition to Laud's and Wentworth's imposition of Arminian ceremonialism on the Irish church.

For most of the time Roman Catholic clergy were left alone and laws against Catholic recusants appeared to be disregarded. Even so, many Catholics had been alienated by Charles, who failed to confirm their rights to hold land. When he was faced with the problem of raising revenue and troops to deal with the rebellious Scots, however, Charles had no hesitation in turning to Ireland for support. Not surprisingly, it was the Catholic native Irish and Old English rather than the Presbyterian New English who responded more positively to the appeal. The campaign against Scotland collapsed too quickly to make Irish intervention necessary on that occasion, but grave misgivings were aroused in England about where the loyalty of the Irish Catholics lay as the gulf between king and parliament widened.

The role of religion in foreign policy

James I had responded to events on the Continent (see above, p. 31) by renewing his efforts to find a Catholic bride for his son Charles to balance the marriage of his daughter to the Protestant Frederick V of the Palatinate in 1613. In so doing he hoped to affirm his impartiality, but parliament, with its strong Puritan membership, was bitterly opposed to this move. At the same time, James (reluctantly) and parliament (rather more enthusiastically) were endeavouring to recover the Palatinate, lost by James's son-in-law in 1620, which made English involvement in the escalating war in central Europe increasingly likely. Unfortunately, parliament appeared unable to separate the religious and political aspects of the conflict, despite James's determination not to become engaged in a war of religion. His chosen strategy was diplomacy, possibly through the agency of Spain.

Then, in 1623, Prince Charles, accompanied by Buckingham, made an extraordinary visit to Spain to 'woo' the Infanta Isabella. But despite making some ill-judged promises to improve the position of the English Catholics, their venture was unsuccessful and they returned home to announce that the 'Spanish match' was off. They were greeted deliriously and became enormously popular with the Protestant population of England, especially when they promoted war against Spain. Negotiations then were opened for a marriage with the French princess, Henrietta Maria. Thus there would be the requisite Catholic marriage, but with a country whose foreign policy often put her in opposition to the rest of Catholic Europe. It was at this point that James died.

Parliament continued in its customary reluctance to provide the necessary money to finance war, especially as the religious concessions offered to Spain by Charles and Buckingham were becoming public knowledge. Charles's popularity with parliament – and, more importantly, his integrity – began to suffer as they started to feel they had been misled regarding his motives to fight the Spanish. Meanwhile, it emerged that the French marriage had promised an improvement in the position of English Catholics without securing French support for English objectives on the Continent. Even worse, English ships loaned to the French were used against the Huguenot (French Protestant) population. When England found herself at war against the French as well as the Spanish, in 1627, she conducted herself dismally. Charles was forced to sue for peace and to adopt diplomatic means to recover the Palatinate – in other words, to follow the path elected by his father. Thereafter, Charles was obliged to rely on those powers most likely to exert the necessary influence to effect the recovery of the Palatinate – that is, Catholic France and/or Spain.

Conclusion

Although Arminianism appeared to have reflected the position of the majority, it was Charles's promotion of Arminian beliefs and practice which was to lead to confrontation. This was because of the way it had been politicised. Arminianism was adopted and manipulated to bolster and justify a monarch increasingly inclined towards absolutism. As a result, instead of representing the majority view, it came to be seen as a minority position, as dangerous as that of the Puritans, albeit of a quite different character. Accordingly, there came a corresponding politicisation of Puritanism. The general consensus which had existed within a largely united Protestant church was becoming increasingly strained.

The showdown had eventually come with the Scots in 1637. It quickly became clear to Charles that he would need proper financial support if he was going to bring the rebellious Scots under control. With surprising ease he was convinced of the wisdom of recalling parliament. They met on 13 April 1640, only to be dissolved the following month. At the same time Convocation assembled and drew up a set of canons to codify and ratify the changes which had been undertaken in the church since 1604. Laud – determined to continue with his plans to restore discipline in the church – was very closely involved in drawing up these canons. He made it clear that none of the changes were contrary to the law or designed to introduce 'popish superstitions'. On the contrary, he maintained, they originated under Edward VI and Elizabeth and had only recently been allowed to lapse.

The 1640 canons also laboured the point that subjects owed not only their duty but also their financial support to their sovereign. Most controversial of all was the so-called 'etcetera oath', which required obedience to all alterations in the church *etcetera*. Although this meant all aspects of church government as they stood in 1640, its terms were so unclear that it was inconceivable that the clergy could swear such a vague oath. It was hardly surprising that when parliament met again in November (the Long Parliament), the Commons declared the canons of 1640 illegal. Unfortunately for Laud, he was held personally responsible for them. The House of Lords ordered his immediate imprisonment and, beginning in March 1641, some of Laud's most objectionable innovations were reversed. With Laud safely out of the way, the anti-Arminian element of the church felt able to reassert themselves. A 'Root and Branch' petition was presented to parliament in 1640, aimed at the root and branches of episcopal government. (A 'Root and Branch' bill was introduced the following year and bishops were excluded from parliament in 1642.) Charles offered no support to his erstwhile executive power in the church and even disassociated himself from the ecclesiastical policies which Laud had discharged on his behalf since 1625.

The frontispiece to Francis Quarles's *The shepherd oracles*. King Charles I is depicted as defending the church against those who wished to attack it at its roots and branches. In what ways does this reflect the concern of those alarmed at the extensive alterations to the English church proposed by the Puritans?

He went on to distance himself from the clergy who had alienated the hearts of his subjects and instead appointed a number of more moderate clergy to vacant posts. Nevertheless, discontent and discord grew and eventually culminated in armed conflict and civil war.

Document case study

4.1 William Laud on ceremonies

Part of an open letter from Laud to Charles I

This I have observed farther, that no one thing hath made conscientious men more wavering in their own minds, or more apt and easy to be drawn aside from the sincerity of religion professed by the Church of England, than the want of uniform and decent order in too many churches of the kingdom . . . It is true, the inward worship of the heart is the great service of God, and no service acceptable without it; but the external worship of God in His Church is the great witness to the world, that our heart stands right in that service of God . . . To deal clearly with your Majesty, these thoughts are they, and no other, which have made me labour so much as I have done for decency and an orderly settlement of the external worship of God in the church; for of that which is inward there can be no witness among men, nor no example for men. Now, no external action in the world can be uniform without some ceremonies; and these in religion, the ancienter they be the better, so they may fit time and place. Too many overburden the service of God, and too few leave it naked. And scarce anything hath hurt religion more in these broken times than an opinion in too many men, that because Rome had thrust some unnecessary and many superstitious ceremonies upon the Church, therefore the Reformation must have none at all; not considering therewith, that ceremonies are the hedge that fence the substance of religion from all the indignities which profaneness and sacrilege too commonly put upon it.

Source: *The works of William Laud*, vol. II, p. xvi, in C. Daniels and J. Morrill, *Charles I*, Cambridge, 1988, pp. 58–59

4.2 Scottish concerns regarding the kirk

From The Scottish National Covenant, 27 February 1638

We noblemen, barons, gentlemen, burgesses, ministers, and commons under subscribing, considering divers times before, and especially at this time, the danger of the true reformed religion of the King's honour, and of the public of the kingdom, by the manifold innovations and evils generally contained and particularly mentioned in our late supplications, complaints, and protestations, do hereby profess, and before God, His angels and the world, solemnly declare, that with our whole hearts we agree and resolve all the days of our life constantly to adhere unto and to defend the aforesaid true religion, and forbearing the practice of all novations already introduced in the matters of the worship of God, or approbation of the corruptions of the public government of the Kirk, or civil places and power of kirkmen, till they be tried and allowed in free assemblies and in Parliaments, to labour by all means lawful to recover the purity and liberty of the Gospel as it was established and professed before the aforesaid novations; and because, after due examination, we plainly perceive and undoubtedly believe that the innovations and evils contained in our supplications, complaints, and protestations have no warrant of the Word of God, are contrary to the articles of the aforesaid confessions, to the intention and meaning of the blessed reformers of religion in this land, to the above-written Acts of Parliament, and do sensibly tend to the re-establishing of the popish religion and tyranny, and to the subversion and ruin of the true reformed religion, and of our liberties, laws and estates . . .

Source: S. R. Gardiner (ed.), *The constitutional documents of the Puritan revolution, 1625–1660*, 3rd edn, Oxford, 1906, p. 132

4.3 English objections to an episcopal church

Part of the preface and a selection of particulars from The London Root and Branch Petition, 11 December 1640

That whereas the government of archbishops and lord bishops . . . have proved prejudicial and very dangerous both to the Church and Commonwealth, they themselves having formerly held that they have their jurisdiction or authority of human authority, till of these later times, being further pressed about the unlawfulness, that they have claimed their calling immediately from the Lord Jesus Christ, which is against the laws of this kingdom, and derogatory to His Majesty and his state royal. And whereas the said government is found by woeful experience to be the main cause and occasion of many foul evils, pressures and grievances of a very high nature unto His Majesty's subjects in their own consciences, liberties and estates, as in a schedule of particulars hereunto annexed may in part appear:

   We therefore most humbly pray, and beseech this honourable assembly, the premises considered, that the said government, with all its dependencies, roots and branches, may be abolished . . .

6. The great increase of idle, lewd and dissolute, ignorant and erroneous men in the ministry, which swarm like the locusts of Egypt over the whole kingdom; and will they but wear a canonical coat, a surplice, a hood, bow at the name of Jesus, and be zealous of superstitious ceremonies, they may live as they list, confront whom they please, preach and vent what errors they will, and neglect preaching at their pleasures without control . . .

10. The publishing and venting of Popish, Arminian, and other dangerous books and tenets; as namely, 'That the Church of Rome is a true Church, and in the worst times never erred in fundamentals;'

11. The growth of Popery and increase of Papists, Priests and Jesuits in sundry places, but especially about London since the Reformation; the frequent venting of crucifixes and Popish pictures both engraven and printed, and the placing of such in Bibles . . .

16. The turning of the Communion-table altar-wise, setting images, crucifixes, and conceits over them, and tapers and books upon them . . . and forcing people to come up thither to receive, or else denying the sacrament to them; terming the altar to be the

mercy-seat, or the place of God Almighty in the church, which is a plain devise to usher in the Mass.

Source: S. R. Gardiner (ed.), *The constitutional documents of the Puritan revolution, 1625–1660*, 3rd edn, Oxford, 1906, pp. 136–41

Document case-study questions

The questions are based on the documents but you may need to look elsewhere in the book for relevant information.

1 How does Laud justify the use of ceremonies in the church in 4.1?

2 What are the concerns expressed by the Scottish Covenanters in 4.2 regarding the future of the kirk?

3 Discuss the grievances and fears of the Root and Branch petitioners in 4.3. Who was their chief target?

4 What are the chief differences expressed in these three documents? How far is a reconciliation of these views possible?

5 The Civil War and the Interregnum

The Civil War, which began in 1642, has been described by historian John Morrill as the last of the wars of religion which blighted Europe in the early modern period. Of course, this is a very simplistic interpretation of an extremely complex situation. As he acknowledges, while it is certainly true that the English Civil War was a war of religion, it was not *only* a war of religion. Also, whereas the Continental religious wars tended to be between Catholics and Protestants, the conflict in England (and Scotland, though not Ireland) was firmly within Protestantism. Even so, because the catalyst for the Civil War had been a point of religious principle, it was inevitable that religious issues would be high on the agenda thereafter. An important development in recent studies of the Civil War has been the greater attention paid to Charles I's unusual position as king of three different countries: England, Scotland and Ireland. Each had very different identities, systems and, crucially, religious positions, and it required a fair degree of flexibility to rule them successfully. Any king was likely to face problems; an intransigent king was bound to.

In fact, the Civil War had its origins in Scotland with Charles's attempts to impose religious uniformity on the Scots: first through the agency of his bishops and then by force, in the First Bishops' War in the summer of 1639. He was obliged to recall his English parliament – after an absence of eleven years – to raise the necessary funds to engage the Scots in a Second Bishops' War, in 1640. The Scots soon gained the upper hand and Charles, in a much weakened position, was faced with vociferous condemnation of his ecclesiastical policy by parliament. Parliament itself had received a number of petitions to abolish bishops, as well as some in their favour. While the king was endeavouring to come to terms with the Scottish Covenanters in Edinburgh in 1641, news arrived in London that the Irish Catholics had risen in revolt and were massacring Protestants. This roughly coincided with allegations of a Royalist plot – the 'Incident' – against the Covenanter leaders. As the English parliament tried to negotiate with the king he 'raised his standard' at Nottingham in August 1642. In other words, he was determined to impose his will on parliament, and civil war began.

Throughout the next four years of civil war, parliament proceeded to dismantle Charles's religious arrangements. A Westminster Assembly of Divines was set up in 1643 to discuss a new church settlement – against the background of a multiplicity of religious sects. It agreed to ban the use of the Book of Common Prayer in 1645, and with parliament's approval it was withdrawn. The following year, parliament abolished bishops. Though the king was defeated in the summer of 1646, for a further two and a half years parliament tried to reach a settlement with Charles. An increasingly militant parliamentary army gradually became less committed to finding a negotiated agreement with an ever more untrustworthy king, and in January 1649 they scraped together sufficient support from a deeply divided, and largely uneasy, parliament to try and then execute King Charles. The next eleven years were known as the Interregnum (i.e. the period between kings). It was a time of confusion and indecision as parliament and the army sought to establish a regime which would replace the monarchy. What everyone desired was a 'godly commonwealth', but there were many different interpretations of what such a state should be and how it was to be achieved and implemented.

Scotland

King Charles had found himself unable to raise the necessary support to subdue the Scots in 1638, partly because of a marked reluctance on the part of many Englishmen to take arms on behalf of the king's drive to inflict his style of church on Scotland. It was resented enough in England and few people wished to be a party to its imposition elsewhere. Charles then made an already contentious situation worse by proposing to enlist the support of the Catholics of the south-west of Scotland, as well as Ireland. His appointment of the crypto-Catholic earl of Arundel to command his army against the Scots, and appeals to Catholic Spain and the English Catholics for financial support for his war effort, damaged his position as protector of the Protestant faith still further. It was hardly surprising, therefore, that support for Charles in the First Bishops' War, against a vastly superior Scottish army, was so inadequate. In June 1639 he was forced to accept a truce. A Scottish parliament and Assembly of the Kirk met to decide on how to restore peace, and promptly confirmed the abolition of the episcopacy, thereby clearly expressing their verdict on Charles's style of church.

When Charles was forced to recall his English parliament, following the defeat of his English troops in the Second Bishops' War in 1640, he discovered that they had religious grievances of their own. As it became clear that the king was not going to bow to any of their demands, relations with the king steadily deteriorated to the point where parliament endeavoured to secure Scottish support in 1641. Their alliance was conditional on a reconstruction of the English church along Scottish-style Presbyterian lines. Even so, the Covenanters were divided about joining the Solemn League and Covenant with the English parliament in 1643. Their misgivings were confirmed when the English parliament came to implement the terms of the agreement with the Scots, after they had helped to secure victory against the king in June 1646. For it soon became clear that there were very wide discrepancies between the different shades of religious opinion regarding their visions of the English church. Efforts to set up a wholly Presbyterian system of church government were resisted vigorously by a considerable proportion of parliament, and it was a very watered-down style of Presbyterianism which eventually was established in 1646.

Curiously, the Scots' best hopes for seeing their interpretation of Presbyterianism adopted in England then became centred on King Charles. After escaping from the custody of the English parliament at the end of 1647, he began making overtures to the more conservative Scots, including a promise to establish a Presbyterian system of church government in England for a three-year trial period. Accordingly, a treaty known as 'The Engagement' was concluded between King Charles and the Scots. The Civil War moved into a second stage as a second Civil War was fought in 1648. In the event, Oliver Cromwell, a leading parliamentarian, together with his New Model Army, dealt with the combined Scottish and royalist initiative with remarkable ease. Thus Cromwell was able to attribute his victories to the hand of God, while Charles's cynical manipulation of the Scots' religious sentiments left him looking altogether unprincipled.

The way in which both the king and parliament professed an interest in Presbyterianism served only to highlight the differences between English and Scottish religious attitudes. It also revealed how far Scotland's concerns were subordinated to English interests by the king and parliament. The Covenanters, who had led the original revolt against the Prayer Book in 1638–41 and then joined the English parliament against the king, disintegrated. Those who later had fought unsuccessfully for the king in the second Civil War – the 'Engagers' – had their property confiscated. Many more of the Scottish elite lost their estates as Scotland became a conquered province of England after 1651. As part of the process of consolidating their victory throughout the 1650s, the English parliament subjected the Scottish church to complete domination. That the Scots were considered of little account regarding the government of their church was plainly demonstrated when the conditions for restoring King Charles II revealed nothing at all about the future of the Scottish church. Its settlement appeared to be almost an afterthought.

Ireland

While Scotland was descending into disarray as a consequence of English interference in its religious affairs, Ireland appeared to be relatively quiet. The Lord Deputy, Thomas Wentworth, had a degree of control over Ireland which Laud and the privy council in England could only dream of. Yet he had achieved this position by aiming his administrative reforms not just at the native Irish, but also at the Old English, or Anglo-Irish (who were largely Catholic), and the New English (the recent Protestant settlers). Thus Wentworth had alienated almost every level of society and shade of religious opinion in Ireland.

When Wentworth was recalled to England to help the king against the Scots, the resentments he had kept in check exploded. In October 1641 the Old English Catholics rose up in rebellion against the New English settlers and committed gross atrocities against them. Reports varied, but the best estimates suggest four thousand Protestants died immediately while a further eight thousand perished when they were thrust from their homes in winter. This revolt confirmed every Anglo-Protestant fear of aggressive Catholicism. In the English parliament, John Pym skilfully took advantage of the atmosphere of plot and murder to urge a limitation on the king's authority and his ability to turn to disreputable advisers, such as Wentworth. Ireland, however, was left to its own devices.

Under the guidance of the Catholic bishops the rebels set up a provisional government – the so-called Confederation of Kilkenny – which resolved to bring about the restoration of Catholicism as the official religion of Ireland. Anglo-Protestant resistance was led by the earl of Ormond, but his position was constantly undermined by Charles, whose only interest in Ireland appeared to be as a source of troops – either Catholic rebel or Protestant loyalist – for his English endeavours. Throughout the 1640s civil war raged in Ireland: usually more concentrated in the north. Catholics were fighting one another as well as the Protestants; pro-royalist Protestant settlers were fighting pro-parliamentarian settlers; both were fighting the Catholics; and everyone was fighting the Scots in Ulster. The violence and slaughter were beyond anything experienced on mainland Britain.

Images such as this showing the massacre of Irish Protestants reached England in 1641–42. What would have been their impact on English Protestants?

There was a temporary respite with the Treaty of Kilkenny in 1649, which guaranteed religious toleration as well as providing for an independent parliament for Ireland. But six months later Cromwell comprehensively conquered Ireland. Beginning with the infamous assaults on Drogheda and then Wexford – ostensibly as retribution for the massacres attributed to the Irish rebels – Ireland was systematically brought under English parliamentary control. By the spring of 1652 the subjugation of Ireland was complete and negotiations began for the drawing up of an Act of Settlement.

To pay for its earlier campaigns in England and Scotland the English parliament had raised loans on Irish rebel lands, so that by 1652 over one thousand English 'Irish Adventurers' held claims on Irish property. In addition, there were soldiers who had been paid partly in cash and partly on the promise of Irish estates. The solution to settling all these claims was devastating in its simplicity: the lands of all Irish Catholics who could not prove their loyalty to the English parliament were confiscated and the Catholics were then herded to an area in the west of Ireland. The pattern of landowning was transformed, as the share of Irish land owned by Catholics dropped from three-quarters to one fifth. At the same time, Protestants replaced Catholics in positions of power in the towns.

Ireland also lost its own parliament and thereafter sent representatives to the Commonwealth parliament in England. Predictably, a Puritan ecclesiastical policy was adopted for Ireland which had at its heart the provision of 'ministers of the gospel' to sow a kind of Presbyterianism throughout Ireland and 'convert' the popish Irish. However, because of the lack of resources and competent ministers, such ambitions were never properly achieved. In the event, these endeavours appear to have done more to unite and stiffen the resolve of the Catholics against the Protestant English.

Varieties of Protestantism in the Civil War

The English parliament which was recalled in November 1640 opened with a speech by Pym. He claimed that there was 'a design to alter law and religion' and declared that there was a conspiracy, or popish plot, afoot. By means of some rather questionable procedures, the king's chief advisers – Laud and Wentworth – were indicted for encouraging Papists in pursuit of their malicious and tyrannical designs on behalf of the king, and, in due course, they were executed. Parliament went on to effect a series of radical reforms of the state and to draw up a *Protestation* in May 1641. This was a nationwide oath to defend the true reformed Protestant church against all popery and popish innovation.

At this stage parliament was still firmly committed to supporting the king against his disreputable advisers. However, Charles's decision to go to Scotland, where his supporters were endeavouring to seize power from the ultra-Presbyterian Covenanters, undermined his stance as the unwitting victim of circumstance. When he attempted to have his leading critics in the English parliament arrested, his position deteriorated still further. Above all, his willingness to consider employing Catholic Irish troops against Scottish

Protestants and his efforts to raise support from Catholic Spain, lost him considerable goodwill. Despite asserting his determination to maintain the Church of England as settled in Queen Elizabeth's reign, the slide towards civil war continued, with the first encounter between the forces of the king and parliament coming in the autumn of 1642.

Yet throughout the civil war years, parliament was deeply divided on several issues – including the future of the English church. There were those who sought a return to the relatively modest Elizabethan religious settlement, constructed on pre-Reformation practices, which position can best be described as 'Anglican'. Then there was a 'Presbyterian' element who looked for a Scottish style, self-determining church, as well as a number of 'Independents' who believed that every congregation should have its own church, governed by itself, but within a loosely organised national church. They took as their model the experiences of those who had fled to the New World (North America). As well as the religious 'Presbyterians' and religious 'Independents', there were also political 'Presbyterians' and 'Independents', who were not necessarily the same as their religious counterparts, which further complicated an already complex and confusing situation.

Parliament's divided vision of the future was clearly illustrated when they tried to find a religious settlement after the first Civil War, in 1646. Their attempts to honour their promise to the Scots, to adopt a wholly Presbyterian system of church government, were obstructed by certain elements within parliament, not least by the Westminster Assembly of Divines, which had been set up to address

What was the chief target of the army in the 'purifying' of English churches during the Civil War? How might the more moderate element of the population have reacted to this iconoclasm?

the future of the church. Also, it emerged that in the turmoil following the breakdown of ecclesiastical discipline many independent churches had been established. These doctrinal Independents had a good measure of support from the army, including, as an early champion, Oliver Cromwell. However, religious opinion within the army was also divided – between those in the lower ranks, who subscribed to the increasingly radical views of the new religious sects, and the more conservative officers, who feared the social change (or revolution) which was implied in many of those radical religious sects.

Catholics

Meanwhile, what of the Catholics? Sustained efforts have been made by historians to establish the number of Roman Catholics in mid-seventeenth-century England. These efforts have been hampered by the fact that, because the widely held fear of an internal Papist rising or plot had contributed so crucially to the outbreak of civil war, it is conceivable that the extent of Catholicism had been exaggerated. Certainly, there was a clear Catholic presence at court and Charles was quite prepared to exploit his Catholic queen's connections for support when faced by rebellion in Scotland. Yet it is very much more difficult to estimate the hold of Catholicism in the country at large.

The breakdown of national government during the Civil War had a knock-on effect throughout the country, which made a particularly powerful impact on the Catholic community. Paradoxically, the one consistent element in the series of attempts to come to terms with the king had been that existing laws against recusants were to be enforced. Consequently, Catholics became easy – even legitimate – targets in the social upheaval of the 1640s. By the 1650s, when, it has been claimed, England had the freest religious climate in the early modern period, only Roman Catholics (together with episcopalian Anglicans) were denied official toleration. On the other hand, it is becoming clear that those who exercised discretion were relatively undisturbed; and it was not the Catholics who tended to attract attention in the Interregnum.

Radicalism

The establishment of a godly commonwealth to replace the institution of the monarchy after January 1649 proved rather more problematic than had been anticipated. To the conservatives among the king's opponents, victory seemed to conclude the 'revolution', whereas for the radicals it was only the beginning. For them, the triumphs of Cromwell's army of saints was the prelude to a new order. A number of religious sects grew up, each dedicated to some kind of political change which seemed threatening to some and visionary to others.

Levellers

The most high-profile sect was the Levellers, who dreamed of a social order organised upon the basis of reason. John Lilburne and other Leveller leaders criticised the unrepresentative nature of England's constitution and the inequalities of the law – especially given that all people were created equal before God. They demanded the disestablishment of the church and the decentralisation of the legal system. To articulate their aspirations they produced an *Agreement of the People* in 1647 (and another in 1649), which proposed a general reconstruction based on a popularly elected annual parliament. In addition, it removed all compulsion from matters of religious faith. The religion of the country was to be as varied as the faiths that existed in it and even Catholics could practise their faith without disturbance. What was contemplated by the *Agreement* was a kind of lower-middle-class utopia. But, although its humani-tarianism – expressed through proposals to care for the poor, the old, the sick, the oppressed and the unemployed – seemed to be an articulation of the Christian message, it was no more than a glorious hope of men who lacked all possibility of gaining power. Although they infiltrated army ranks, the Levellers were unwilling to subscribe to violence as a tactic, and they had little hope of converting the established authorities by persuasion, given that they so plainly threatened their interests. Cromwell, on the other hand, had no such qualms about resorting to force, and so it was his vision – of an oligarchic (government by a few) rather than a democratic republic – which was realised.

Fifth Monarchists

The Fifth Monarchy men were very different from the Levellers. Their movement developed out of Millenarian Utopianism – a creed which was based on the belief that Jesus Christ's one-thousand-year reign was imminent, after which Christ would appear to judge the world and bring it to an end. King Jesus's reign was to be conducted by his saints, who were, of course, the Fifth Monarchy men. Once in power, the Fifth Monarchists would sweep away such evils as tithes and corrupt lawyers, and effect other social reforms. They differed from the Levellers in their fundamental belief, based on their Puritan emphasis on the believer's inward grace, that this was to be achieved through a theocracy of saints and not by general suffrage. Their whole doctrine rested on their conviction that, in Christ's Kingdom, Scripture would be the only law. Thus they carried Puritan biblical literalism to such fanatical extremes that they made their success an impossibility.

At first the Fifth Monarchists believed that Cromwell (whom they compared to Moses) was the first of the saints. But, while they were more firmly supported by Colonel Thomas Harrison, who had been active in debating the *Agreement of the People*, and others in the army who subscribed to their view that the time had come to break down earthly powers, Cromwell was more conservative and urged caution. Harrison and his followers were gradually purged from positions of power, and when Cromwell assumed the role of Lord Protector in 1653 the Fifth Monarchists felt utterly betrayed.

Diggers

The Diggers were a movement founded by Gerrard Winstanley, who developed the idea of a communist Utopia. He had adopted a series of religious and political positions, in quick succession, before leading the Diggers at the beginning of 1649 to cultivate the common lands on St George's Hill in Surrey. Claiming that this concept had come to him while in a trance, he concluded that reason and righteousness were manifest in the common ownership of the earth. Winstanley emphasised that such a society was not to be instituted by force, but would come about because all people would naturally consent to the law of reason. Meanwhile, he led his little group of followers in their communist experiment – working the common lands, and patiently awaiting the rich to voluntarily give up their property and goods. His final writing, *The law of freedom* (1652), was a detailed plan for a communist order: money and private property would be banned; its administration was to be by annually elected officials; schools were to provide vocational and academic education; and religious observances were to take the form of Sunday discourses (or discussions).

Inevitably, the Digger communes attracted the wrath of all property-owners and their days were numbered. Within a year or so they were gone. At the same time, the Levellers were reduced to little more than pamphleteers. Their brief association with Cromwell lasted only as long as it suited his purposes. Their aspirations were quite contrary to his own interests and the connection was dissolved at the earliest opportunity. Following the imprisonment of some of its leaders, an increasingly disillusioned movement gradually ground to a halt. Yet all these shattered dreams belonged to only a very few, for it has been estimated that the radical sects probably never attracted more than 5 per cent of the English population. Nevertheless, they represent a unique period in English religious (and social) history when almost anything seemed possible.

Conclusion

In the aftermath of the Civil War, the conservative majority were not looking for the kind of solutions offered by the proliferation of radical religious sects. Whilst applauding the dismantling of traditional structures of authority within the church, particularly the episcopate, they feared and condemned challenges to the existing social order. This was reflected in Cromwell's efforts to achieve a 'godly reformation' through an alliance of godly magistrates and a reformed, educated ministry. For example, in 1650 an Act was passed for the propagation of the gospel in Wales. Yet the Puritan vision turned out to be as constricted as that which it sought to replace, for while 1650 also saw the repeal of the Act of Uniformity, a blasphemy Act against religious nonconformity was passed in the same year. Moreover, as well as promoting predestination doctrine, the Puritan design went much further. It meant strict sabbatarianism and the suppression or prohibition of traditional festivities and rites of passage. Singing and dancing, in their view, were abominations in the sight of the Lord. The popular image of the Puritan kill-joy was born as theatres were closed and Christmas pudding and dancing round the maypole were outlawed. Between 1655 and 1657, the enforcement of these measures was the responsibility of the 'major-generals', who were appointed as moral guardians to oversee local government and monitor behaviour. Though they were never as odious as their enemies claimed, they were, nevertheless, deeply unpopular agents of moral control. So that, despite the broad and tolerant nature of the Cromwellian church, it was the severity of the Calvinist cultural experiment which contributed to the Puritan revolution being so short-lived.

Document case study

5.1 The Levellers' proposals for a religious settlement

From An Agreement of the Free People of England, tendered as a peace-offering to this distressed nation by Lieutenant Colonel John Lilburne, Master William Walwyn, Master Thomas Prince, and Master Richard Overton, prisoners in the Tower of London, 1 May 1649

> *. . . And accordingly we do declare and publish
> to all the world, that we are agreed as follows,*

. . . X. That we do not impower or intrust our said representatives to continue in force, or to make any laws, oaths, or covenants, whereby to compel by penalties or otherwise any person or any thing in or about matters of faith, religion or God's worship or to restrain any person from the profession of his faith, or exercise of religion according to his conscience, nothing having caused more distractions, and heart burnings in all ages, than persecution and molestation for matters in and about religion . . .

. . . XXIV. That it shall not be in their power to impose ministers upon any of the respective parishes, but shall give free liberty to the parishioners of every particular parish, to choose such as themselves shall approve; and upon such terms, and for such reward, as themselves shall be willing to contribute, or shall contract for. Provided, none shall be choosers but such as are capable of electing representatives . . .

. . . XXVI. They shall not disable any person from bearing any office in the common-wealth, for any opinion or practice in religion, excepting such as maintain the popes (or other foreign) supremacy.

Source: William Haller and Godfrey Davies (eds.), *The Leveller tracts 1647–1653*, Columbia, 1944, pp. 318–19, 323, 326

5.2 How the Fifth Monarchy men justify their position

. . . when God awakens the saints and witnesses to hearken to a voice from heaven, that is, from the churches, saying *Come up hither,* Rev. 11.12. when they are content to forget their old forms of government, civil and ecclesiastical, called the *first Heavens, and first Earth,* Rev. 21.1. Isa. 65.17. when I say the saints are come to this pitch, and they will have no laws, statutes, or rules of government in the church or civil state, but what Christ hath given in his word, even from thenceforth does this fifth Monarchy begin, which *Peter* calls the *new Heavens, and new Earth, wherein dwells righteousness,* 2 Pet.

6 The Restoration

King Charles II was restored to the throne on 8 May 1660. The scenes of wild jubilation which greeted his entry into London on 30 May moved him to remark, somewhat sardonically, that it was plainly his own fault he had stayed away for so long. It used to be thought by Restoration historians that the failure of the Puritan revolution marked the end of religion as an important issue, as politics became increasingly secularised. However, a recent conference of Anglo-American historians concluded that, 'it will never be possible again to write about the history of any period without putting religion near the very centre of the picture'. This is as true about the Restoration period as any other.

The Restoration settlement

Thus, the Restoration settlement was as much concerned with the future of the church as with the constitution, relations between crown and parliament, finance, land, trade and foreign policy. While still in exile, Charles had issued a statement or political manifesto called The Declaration of Breda, which confirmed his commitment to 'the Protestant religion' and included a reassuring promise of 'liberty to tender consciences'. However, the Restoration of the monarchy was likely to mean the restoration of a church of England founded firmly upon the Prayer Book and presided over by bishops. The king's chief adviser, Edward Hyde (later earl of Clarendon), worked with the king to find a settlement which could accommodate Presbyterians into an essentially Anglican Church. Accordingly, in October 1660, Charles published the conclusions of a conference held at Worcester House to address the future of the church. The Worcester House Declaration aimed to reconcile Presbyterians with the episcopate and several Presbyterian ministers were appointed as royal chaplains.

But this accord between Anglicans and moderate Presbyterians was not intended to include either radical Protestants or Roman Catholics. The contrast between the broad-based, tolerant church of the Cromwellian period and that which was restored in the early 1660s was made very plain by the series of repressive statutes passed by the Cavalier Parliament, which first met in 1661. Its conservative and intolerant nature was demonstrated by the Corporation Act (1661), which imposed strict religious tests on potential borough office-holders, by the first Conventicles Act (1664), which made attendance at church services that did not conform to the Prayer Book (revised by Convocation in 1662) illegal, and by the Five Mile Act (1665), which effected an exclusion zone around all urban centres on preachers who did not swear to uphold Anglican ideals. A new Act of Uniformity (1662) had imposed the use of a revised version of the Prayer Book – ostensibly drawn up to meet Puritan criticisms but actually even less acceptable than the old – and demanded unequivocal acceptance of its content, by all ministers of the church. The Act also insisted that the principle of rebellion be denied. As a result of the Act of Uniformity a number of Anglican clergy left their parishes.

These measures, known as the Clarendon Code, fully confirmed the primacy of the Anglican Church and excluded even the more moderate Presbyterians from the established Church of England. But the Anglican Church of the 1660s was not the same as the Anglican Church of the 1630s. In some respects there appeared to be little difference: ritual and ceremony were revived and revitalised; church lands and revenues were recovered; the bishops were restored to the House of Lords; and church courts were reactivated. On the other hand, the church no longer made claims of supremacy in the secular sphere. In other words, the provocative politicisation of the Laudian or Caroline church was not a part of the Restoration recovery. For instance, whereas the church courts had jurisdiction over spiritual matters, it was left to the gentry, in their capacity as JPs, to punish moral miscreants.

The triumph of narrow, High Anglicanism seemed to ignore Charles II's promises regarding liberty for tender consciences made immediately before his Restoration. In fact, the Restoration settlement of the church carried with it significant implications for the king, for the church had been re-established on the initiative of parliament, who articulated the aspirations of the bishops and the gentry. Thus, the arrangements contained an implicit challenge to the king's religious supremacy. King Charles determined to exert his authority by issuing a Declaration of Indulgence, which offered toleration to all loyal though dissenting subjects in December 1662. It was successfully opposed by parliament.

Nonconformity and persecution

The Restoration settlement of the church brought to an end the latitude enjoyed by many of the religious groups during the 1650s and there followed almost thirty years of persecution. It is difficult to gauge the extent of religious dissent in the reign of Charles II: figures compiled for different purposes vary widely and estimates range from around 3 to 20 per cent of the population. The continued existence of such divergent nonconformist sects as Quakers, Baptists and even the more radical Presbyterians was attributed to the fact that an increasingly narrow state church was isolated from the ordinary people in the country, whose spiritual needs were not met by Anglicanism. Their survival demonstrated the way in which minorities tend to thrive under pressure. Recent (and belated) research, on the other hand, has begun to challenge the stereotypical view of an elitist and conservative Anglican Church to which the nation subscribed by default. Instead, it is becoming clear that Anglicanism was developing a vigorous style of its own, which may have had a wider and more positive appeal than once was thought.

The effectiveness of the Clarendon Code in imposing religious conformity depended upon the will of those required to enforce it. Authorities in both town and countryside tended to adopt an attitude which has been described as 'benign neglect' for, on the whole, magistrates were not convinced by official portraits of dissenters as seditious subversives. Also, nonconformists did not present a uniform problem to the civil authorities. Many were simply unable to come to terms with doctrinal elements of Anglicanism but were quite prepared to make an outward show of conformity. For example, Presbyterians attended both the parish church and their own meetings. Others, such as Baptists and Quakers, were quite unable to compromise their beliefs, and it was they who tended to attract the wrath of the state.

King Charles II did not give up after the failure of his Declaration of Indulgence in 1662. There were several further attempts to bring about a toleration of dissenters (and Catholics) but the mood of the Cavalier Parliament was implacable and they all came to nothing. A second Declaration of Indulgence, issued by Charles in 1672, was cancelled the following year. Not until the reign of Charles's brother James (1685–88) did conditions improve for dissenters. With the help of William Penn, a leading Quaker, another Declaration of Indulgence was drafted and issued in 1687 which suspended all penal laws, including the Test and Corporation Acts. But James's Roman Catholic faith meant that any suggestion of relaxing conditions for his dissenting Protestant subjects aroused deep suspicions that he intended making similar concessions to the Catholics. King James's wish to repeal the penalties against Catholicism eventually led to his downfall and he was replaced by his son-in-law, the Protestant Dutch prince, William of Orange. This augured very well for all nonconformists for William of Orange was a Calvinist who was not prepared to be dictated to by the Anglicans. The first year of his reign saw the passing of the Toleration Act (1689) and, at last, Protestant dissenters were free to worship openly in their own meeting houses.

Catholics

The proportion of the population who held to their Catholic faith was probably fairly constant throughout the period covered by this book. This was despite the papal missions regularly dispatched from the Continent to swell Catholic numbers and the corresponding attempts by the state to reduce them. Another constant factor was the kind of informal toleration shown to them by those expected to implement the penal laws periodically enacted to contain Catholics. In times of crisis, however, anti-Catholic sentiments were all too easily aroused. When it seemed as if Catholicism was gaining ground at the centre, especially at court, these passions could become violent and even hysterical. King Charles II was widely suspected of being sympathetic to Catholicism (if not actually a Catholic) and his brother, the duke of York (the future King James II), was openly a Catholic after 1673.

Throughout the Restoration period efforts to secure toleration for Protestant dissenters were accompanied by endeavours to achieve similar liberties of conscience for Roman Catholics. These came to an abrupt end when James, duke of York, announced his conversion to Catholicism. The prospect of a Catholic king stirred memories of Queen Mary's reign and boded ill for good English Protestants. There was a spate of anti-Catholic pamphleteering and in 1673 parliament passed the Test Act. This required all office-holders to sign a declaration against transubstantiation, one of the chief doctrinal planks of Catholicism. James's marriage to a Catholic princess raised anti-Catholic feelings almost to fever pitch. Local magistrates swung into action against Catholic recusants and efforts were redoubled to exclude Catholics from positions of power in central government.

Rumours of popish treachery proliferated throughout the 1670s. Then, in 1678, came Titus Oates and his disclosure of a popish plot to end all popish plots. He claimed that Jesuits (disguised as Fifth Monarchy men!) were inciting Catholics to revolt and massacre London's Protestant population before destroying the city. The climax of the plot was to be the assassination of the king. The narrative was lavishly embellished with details designed to inflame anti-Catholic passions and, predictably, fear of popery swept the country. The veracity of Oates's story was highly questionable but a recent verdict on the popish plot concludes that the significance of the 'plot' lies in the fact that emotions were so easily whipped-up on such flimsy evidence, thus implying an abiding and deep-seated hostility to Catholicism in the English psyche.

By the spring of 1679 most of the fears engendered by the popish plot had subsided, but not before the government had ordered that all laws against Catholics were to be enforced with increased rigour, and parliament passed a Second Test Act (1678) which excluded Catholics from both Houses of Parliament. However, when efforts were made to pass a bill to disinherit (i.e. exclude from the succession) James, duke of York, King Charles dissolved parliament in January 1679. Further efforts to get an Exclusion Bill through the next parliaments were also unsuccessful, though the fact that the parliaments from 1679 to 1681 were designated Exclusion Parliaments indicates that it was the dominant matter under discussion.

The role of religion in party politics

An enduring legacy of the Exclusion Crisis, arising from the debates about the Exclusion Bill, was its contribution to the birth of national party politics. Those members who promoted the exclusion of the Catholic duke of York from the succession were known first as 'exclusionists', then as 'petitioners' and eventually as Whigs. Their parliamentary opponents – or anti-exclusionists – were labelled as Tories. The latter quickly learned from the successful electioneering tactics pioneered by the Whigs, and organised themselves as the defenders of the monarchy and champions of the High Anglican Church which was implacably opposed to toleration either for dissenting Protestants or for

See here the Dauils Darling, plotting still
With Blood & Treasons all y̆. world to fill.
His Romish stratagems, Loe, Non can tell
Who cãnot fathom to y̆.Depth of Hell.
Nothing but Murder'd Kings can him suffice
And flaming Citys as a Sacrifice

Yet see behind his chaire Whom Heav'n̆s ent,
Whom God hath made a timely Instrument
Englands intended ruine to prevent
That which, y̆.Devil & y̆.Pope combin'd
Against our King and Protestants decign'd
Disclos'd and frustrated by him wee find.

Pope.

Oates

The Emblem Explayn'd

AA the Popes Cabbinett.

B {the Pope writing to the Jesuits to
{be diligent in the careing on the Plott.

C {Mr. Oats who unseene lokes ouer his
{sholder & sees all his Contriuances.

D {the Popes Crone who cries friend
{Oates is behind you.

E {the Popes title of Supremacie falling
{donne accasioned by his Sudaine Motion.

F {a Blott which his Surprise made him
{fall vpon y̆. worke Roman in his Letter.

G {a croune Mr. Oates giues him more fit
{for his Head then the former.

A print illustrating the pope's shock at discovering that the latest Catholic conspiracy has been exposed by Titus Oates, in 1678. How does this demonstrate the Protestants' conviction that Catholic plots were either instigated by the pope or contrived with full papal approval?

Catholics. The Tories took full advantage of the uncertain atmosphere in the aftermath of the Exclusion Crisis to cast the Whigs as dissenters and republicans, and joined with the king to assert royal authority based on an alliance of monarchy and the Church of England.

When James eventually became king, in 1685, he found himself in harmony with the Whigs precisely because of their dissenting sympathies. A Whig majority in the House of Commons, James believed, could be relied upon to repeal the penal laws against all recusants – both nonconformists and Catholics. This seriously alarmed the Anglican Tories, who made cautious overtures to William of Orange. Matters began to reach crisis point when plans were revealed to force the Anglican clergy to sanction toleration for dissenters by publicly approving the second Declaration of Indulgence issued in 1688. The so-called Seven Bishops' Case, involving the arrest of six bishops and William Sancroft, archbishop of Canterbury, who expressed misgivings at this latest turn of events, added to the general dismay. Protestant suspicions appeared to be confirmed when a disproportionate number of Catholics were appointed to important local offices. The abiding parallels drawn between Roman Catholicism and absolute monarchical government – coupled with the prospect of another Catholic king after the queen gave birth to a son – drove a cross-party bloc to invite the Protestant Dutch ruler William of Orange to come and save England from its Catholic fate.

The role of religion in foreign policy

William's willingness to consider invading England was part of his lifelong determination to check the ambitions of the king of France. Since 1670 England had been implicated in those ambitions by virtue of a treaty made with France – ostensibly to join in an offensive war against the Dutch Republic – which carried with it very significant religious implications. In fact, there were two versions of this treaty, known as the Treaty of Dover. Both versions agreed that France would pay a considerable sum of money to England (a war subsidy) but one of them also contained a secret clause whereby King Charles II would declare his conversion to Catholicism in return for a substantial financial 'bonus', when the time was ripe.

On the face of it, an alliance with Catholic France against Protestant Holland might have been difficult to justify, but there were very sound economic reasons for England to engage in a war against their long-time commercial rivals, the Dutch. But the war went badly and English opinion began to question the wisdom of an alliance with France. With Charles II calling for a suspension of the penal laws against Catholics (as well as Protestant dissenters), and James, duke of York, announcing in 1673 his conversion to Catholicism, suspicions were aroused about Charles's own religious position. There was also widespread concern about the political and absolutist nature of Catholicism, especially as it was developing in France, and Charles's inclination to emulate the style of kingship adopted by the king of France.

Even when Thomas Danby, the king's new chief minister, pursued anti-French and pro-Dutch policies in 1674, which included the marriage of James's Protestant daughter to William of Orange, rumours and distrust persisted. For instance, it was believed by many that Charles intended to use the standing army to rule England without parliament. It was at this point that the popish plot and the Exclusion Crisis flared up and attention was temporarily turned inwards. By the time of James II's reign, however, events on the Continent were once again to have dramatic consequences for England. Not the least of these were the invasion of England by William of Orange and James II's subsequent flight to France.

Scotland

Formal decisions regarding the future of the Scottish church after the Restoration of Charles II were taken in London, albeit on the advice of those who claimed to represent the different shades of opinion in Scotland. What was finally settled upon was an episcopal church – sometimes called episcopacy-in-presbytery – which was similar to the Anglican Church, but with a distinctly Scottish character. At the same time, the Lords of the Articles (a committee appointed by the crown which met before parliament sat in order to decide the agenda) agreed that parliament should annul all acts passed by the Scottish parliament since 1633, including the legislation which had guaranteed the existence of the Presbyterian Church. An episcopacy was restored. There followed the prohibition of conventicles, or 'illegal' assemblies, and a period of persecution or repression ensued as Presbyterian ministers were ejected from their livings.

The so-called Pentland Rising of 1666 (which actually originated at the opposite end of Scotland from Pentland) was ostensibly in reaction to the severe repression of the kirk. In fact, limited toleration of nonconformity was already being promoted, especially by the secretary for Scotland, the earl of Lauderdale, and it might be said that the Pentland Rising merely quickened its pace. However, the kirk became over-confident and, as the number of conventicles increased, the state reverted to its policy of repression, and a further Act against conventicles was passed in 1670. Presbyterian resentment finally boiled over into another rebellion, culminating in the murder of the archbishop of St Andrews in 1679, which was put down relatively easily by English troops. Curiously, the reign of James II (VII of Scotland) was something of a comfort to the Presbyterians, who profited from his policy of toleration, which extended to Protestant dissenters as well as to Catholics. However, as James was soon embroiled in the conflict with William of Orange, it was never put to the test how far the Presbyterians would continue to benefit from James's 'liberal' religious policies.

Ireland

In Ireland, as well as in England and Scotland, the return of the monarchy presaged a restoration of an episcopal form of a state church – in other words, a Church of Ireland organised along similar lines to that established by the

Restoration settlement in England. At the same time, because many Catholics had fought for the royalist cause in Ireland, they confidently looked forward to toleration of their faith and recovery of their lands. For the Presbyterians, who had prospered during the Cromwellian period, the Restoration meant they faced marginalisation by an Anglican Church while their territorial gains were at risk. Efforts by the Irish parliament to solve the insoluble land problem produced an Act of Settlement, in 1661, which was so infeasible it provoked the following, often quoted, remark from the Lord Lieutenant, Lord Ormond: 'there must be new discoveries made of a new Ireland, for the old will not serve to satisfy these engagements'. A second, more realistic Act, the Act of Explanation, was passed four years later. This was distinctly more favourable to the Protestants than the Catholics, and was to cause continued resentment and agitation for its repeal.

The Protestants may have gone some way to securing their property rights but there was no such certainty for the Presbyterians and other Protestant dissenters regarding their religion. For them the establishment of an Anglican Church had serious implications. Presbyterians were excluded from national and local politics, they could not hold public office, and their ministers began to be evicted. On the other hand, the ramifications of the Restoration were much more positive for the Catholics. In 1662 a Remonstrance (i.e. a declaration of loyalty) was drawn up to distinguish between loyal and disloyal Papists, thus making Catholicism no longer necessarily synonymous with treason. Thereafter, the Catholics enjoyed a kind of unofficial tolerance which meant that Roman Catholic clergy could minister to their flocks, schools and monasteries were founded, and the mass was openly celebrated. The pope even appointed a titular archbishop of Dublin, who led the efforts to repeal the Acts of Settlement and Explanation. Yet the Catholics were still subject to changes in official attitude, while episodes of hysteria associated with popery in England inevitably had repercussions in Ireland. Though conditions for the Catholics undoubtedly improved with the Restoration of the monarchy, the period was nevertheless one of uncertainty and anxiety.

The accession of James II seemed to promise much more to the Irish Catholics, especially after he appointed the Catholic earl of Tyconnel as Lord Lieutenant. Tyconnel began a policy of aggressive Catholicisation by purging the army of Protestant officers and increasing the number of Roman Catholic judges and privy councillors. Although the Church of Ireland was not disestablished, it began to decline, as revenues went astray and vacancies were left unfilled. The Irish parliament which met in 1689 was dominated by Catholics. They pledged their support for King James, whose throne had been under threat since William of Orange had landed in England in 1688. Only the Protestants in Ulster proclaimed William as king.

It was to be in Ireland that the conflict between Catholic James and Protestant William was resolved. In the Irish context the ensuing war was one of a stark struggle between Protestant and Catholic. For both James and William, however, not only was it significant in determining possession of the throne of England but it also carried far wider, European considerations. For whereas James was

7 The Glorious Revolution and beyond

For a second time in the seventeenth century, a king of England, Scotland and Ireland had lost his throne. In both instances the loss was due to the belief that the king meant to adopt the kind of absolutist royal powers which were associated with Roman Catholicism. Also, both kings were ousted by Protestant regimes of the Puritan, or Calvinist, variety. However, whereas in the 1630s and 1640s Puritanism and nascent Anglicanism were polarised, by 1688–89 they had been driven together in their opposition to the Catholic 'menace'. Hopes were high that this presaged a more comprehensive Protestant church which would either accommodate, or at the very least tolerate, all shades of Protestant opinion.

Protestants

In the event the opportunity was lost. With the threat of popery removed, Protestant unity collapsed and, of the ambitious legislation hoped for from parliament, only a very limited Toleration Act became law in 1689. In effect it meant that while dissenters could practise their religion without fear of disturbance, they were still subject to a range of penalties. Some of these, such as the requirement for their meeting places to be licensed, were minor irritations, which did not deter more than three and a half thousand applications for licences over the next twenty years or so. More significantly, nonconformists continued to be excluded from public office unless they accepted the Anglican sacraments, according to the Test Acts of 1673 and 1678.

Anglican supremacy was by no means unassailable, though. This was partly because the Church of England was divided within itself and partly because in the latter half of the seventeenth century a more liberal and conciliatory element in the Anglican Church was making its presence felt. They were known as Latitudinarians. At the heart of their beliefs was the conviction that there was sufficient common ground among all Protestants to unite them against the threat of popery and that their similarities rather than their differences should be emphasised. Thus there was within the Anglican Church an important force in favour of accommodating, and working with, other Protestant sects. In many ways they anticipated the rational views of the late seventeenth and early eighteenth centuries, which found expression in the Age of Reason.

The divide in the English church was accentuated when a number of High Anglican Church leaders, who could not accept the revolutionary nature (Glorious or otherwise) of the events of 1689, were replaced in important church positions by Low Church Latitudinarians. Even the archbishopric of Canterbury was held successively by two Latitudinarian divines (ministers) – John Tillotson (1691–94) and Thomas Tenison (1695–1715). Yet they never realised the comprehensive church for which they strived, because High Church Anglicans continued to be in the majority in the country at large. The position of the latter promised to improve after the accession of Queen Anne in 1702. For unlike her brother-in-law, the Calvinist King William, and her Catholic father, King James II, Anne was an Anglican. But in the event the High Church Anglicans were no more successful than their Low Church rivals in seeing their ambitions realised.

The High Church Anglicans, together with their Tory allies in parliament, aimed at closing the loophole whereby dissenters could appear to conform by once in a while attending Church of England services – in other words, making a show of occasional conformity. Their cause was promoted vociferously by Dr Henry Sacheverell, whose emotive and inflammatory sermons, which identified dissent with republicanism, whipped up considerable popular support. Even so, the proposed legislation to deal with the issue of 'occasional conformity' by prospective office-holders failed to materialise. Between January 1702 and December 1704 three Occasional Conformity Bills were defeated in the House of Lords, where the Whigs were in the majority. Religion continued to polarise Whigs and Tories as each sought to occupy the moral high ground. It was the Tory attack on the Whig's 'Revolution Principles' that brought things to a head. These principles were the rationale which underpinned the Glorious Revolution and justified deposing a lawfully constituted monarch. Once again, Sacheverell was the principal Tory High Church mouthpiece, and he became the chief target of the Whigs. But though Sacheverell was tried and convicted for inciting unrest in his celebrated sermon of 1709, the riots which accompanied the episode, in 1710, were blamed upon the Whigs. The Tories took the opportunity to push through an Occasional Conformity Bill, outlawing occasional conformity, which became law in December 1711.

The Tory triumph was short-lived. On the death of Anne, in 1714, the throne passed to the Lutheran elector of Hanover, who became King George I. No longer was the Tory High Church Anglican position identical to that of the monarch. Some of them even considered inviting James II's son (James Stuart, the Catholic 'Old Pretender') to be king. This became a reality in 1715, when there was a rebellion in his favour. Thus a small minority of hitherto unequivocally loyal Tories found themselves branded as Jacobite rebels.

Catholics

James II's Catholicising policies provoked opposition among his Protestant subjects. To begin with, resistance tended to be passive as parliament refused to repeal the penal laws (see p. 67), while in the localities, Protestants refused to co-operate with Catholics who held important offices. Later, as concerns about James's intentions grew, opposition became more resolute. In particular, there were fears that James might consider following the king of France in his decision to outlaw, and then expel, his Protestant (Huguenot) subjects. A determined pamphleteering campaign fuelled anti-Catholic sentiment, which found expression in sporadic incidents of violence against Catholic chapels and priests.

William of Orange promised an end to disorder as well as to popery and absolutism. Paradoxically, it seemed that the popish threat emanated almost entirely from the king and it was only when popery was politicised that problems arose. Thus, when the Catholic King James II began displaying worrying signs of adopting the absolutist tendencies associated in the English mind with Catholicism, and imposing them on the country at large, suspicions flared. However, when the situation was viewed dispassionately, after the panic had subsided, it was clear that the Catholic community was small and that it was not harbouring ambitions to effect the return of England to Rome. English Protestants could, and did, live peaceably with their Catholic neighbours, and they continued to do so. By the eighteenth century, Catholics were relatively free from persecution. Nevertheless, the century began with the passing of the Act of Settlement, in 1701, which ensured that the throne of England could only be occupied by a communicant member of the Church of England.

Scotland

Whereas the role of the Scots in the downfall of King Charles I had been crucial, their involvement in the expulsion of James II was negligible. Nevertheless, they took full advantage of the Glorious Revolution, in favour of the Calvinist King William, to abandon episcopacy and reinstate those ministers who had been ejected as a consequence of the Restoration settlement of the 1660s. The crown-appointed Lords of the Articles (see above, p. 68) were abolished and the Scottish parliament restored Presbyterian government in the church. In 1690, a General Assembly of the Kirk met for the first time since 1653 and triumphantly confirmed the re-establishment of Presbyterianism in Scotland.

But, contrary to popular belief, the events of 1690 did not signify a Presbyterian Church which was independent of the state. Indeed, a recent verdict on the role of the Scottish church concludes that, as the question of a more complete union with England loomed, in 1706–07, the Scottish church became just another 'interest group' in politics. Accordingly, they sought and were granted guarantees for Presbyterianism in the Act of Union of 1707. Yet within five years the new British parliament legislated in favour of episcopalians, in the 1712 Scottish Toleration Act, which allowed them freedom of worship. Despite the fact that the Union was neither legal nor ecclesiastical, the earlier gains made by the Presbyterians were subject to a serious challenge as a consequence of it.

Ireland

While the Glorious Revolution was welcomed by a significant proportion of the Scottish population, it was a disaster for the majority of the Irish. Initially the thrust of the Treaty of Limerick, which brought to an end the war between King

James and King William, was generous to the Catholics. But Protestant opposition – which threatened to divert William's attention from his Continental objectives (curbing French expansion) – successfully diluted its terms. Accordingly, the Irish parliament which met in 1692 passed a comprehensive series of anti-Catholic laws, intended permanently to subordinate the Catholics, both socially and politically. It has been pointed out that Ireland was unique in western Europe for its persecution of the majority of its people. Although Protestants in France and Spain, for example, were subject to similarly harsh laws, they only ever constituted a minority of the French or Spanish populations.

In the aftermath of the Glorious Revolution, penal laws were enacted to exclude Roman Catholics from parliament, local government, the law and the army. They were still able to advance themselves in trade and industry but their land-holding rights were eroded by laws passed in 1704 and 1709. At a practical level, conditions for Irish Catholics were crippling, and they remained so. On the other hand, the penal laws against religious worship were more difficult to enforce and, for most of the time, they were seldom executed. Yet it was not just Roman Catholics who suffered as a consequence of the Glorious Revolution. Protestant nonconformists – Calvinists and Presbyterians – were also subordinated to the Church of Ireland and liable for payment of tithes towards the established church. These tithes were not abolished until the 1830s.

Papists, Protestants, Puritans and new philosophies

At the beginning of the sixteenth century everyone was a member of one universal 'Catholic' church and, while they did not necessarily share precisely the same set of beliefs or follow exactly the same patterns of devotion, Christianity was common to all. The Christian church was headed by the pope in Rome. Throughout the century, in England, Scotland and Ireland (as well as in certain countries on the Continent), the state assumed control of the church, ostensibly in order to oversee its reform. Thereafter a number of different paths were followed to correct its deficiencies and effect its improvement for ministering the mysteries of religion to the faithful. In England, Scotland and Ireland the process reached a climax in the middle of the seventeenth century with the proliferation of religious sects, each of which offered solutions – to a range of perceived problems – based upon re-ordering society.

Almost every re-think about religion throughout the sixteenth and seventeenth centuries was at the expense of those holding a different set of beliefs. In England, Scotland and Ireland, these were either Protestants who did not conform to the established Church of England (Scotland or Ireland), or Roman Catholics. The government soon became adept at exploiting those whose religious practices were contrary to those prescribed by the state. For example, the economic potential of the Catholics was recognised by James I's privy council as they grappled with the problems of Protestant nonconformist (i.e. Puritan) and Catholic minorities. The Lord Treasurer was quick to point out that whereas the

Puritans brought only strife, the Catholics provided a healthy financial injection into the exchequer in the form of recusancy fines. At another level, by virtue of their exclusion from participating in public life, members of religious minorities turned to trade and industry, where they made a valuable contribution to their country's economic prosperity. Thus, while France lost a vital section of artisans and manufacturers when they expelled the Huguenots in the second half of the seventeenth century, England, Scotland and Ireland benefited by offering them refuge.

After years of struggle against Protestant nonconformists and Roman Catholics, the end of the seventeenth century witnessed a further shift as the church was subject to challenge from a quite different direction: the development of science and scientific methods brought with it a new philosophy which demanded a more rational approach to all beliefs – including belief in God. Although, to begin with, these new scientific theories were always carefully fitted into a Christian framework, the church had to deal with Deism and other examples of free-thinking which questioned its traditional teaching. However, not even the full intellectual weight of the Age of Reason, or the Enlightenment, in the eighteenth century, when some thinkers began to flirt with atheism, ever seriously threatened the confidence and hegemony of the Christian church.

Document case study

7.1 Legislation for limited toleration of Protestant nonconformists

Part of the Toleration Act, 1689

X. And whereas there are certain other persons, dissenters from the Church of England, who scruple the taking of any oath, be it enacted . . . that every such person shall make and subscribe . . . this declaration of fidelity following, viz.,

I, A. B., do sincerely promise and solemnly declare before God and the world that I will be true and faithful to King William and Queen Mary, and I do solemnly profess and declare that I do from my heart abhor, detest and renounce as impious and heretical that damnable doctrine and position that princes excommunicated or deprived by the Pope or any authority of the see of Rome may be deposed or murthered by their subjects or any other whatsoever, and I do declare that no foreign prince, person, prelate, state or potentate hath or ought to have any power, jurisdiction, superiority, pre-eminence or authority, ecclesiastical or spiritual, within this realm.

And shall subscribe a profession of their Christian belief in these words,

I, A. B., profess faith in God the Father, and in Jesus Christ his Eternal Son, the true God, and in the Holy Spirit, one God blessed for evermore, and do acknowledge the Holy Scriptures of the Old and New Testament to be given by divine inspiration.

And every such person that shall make and subscribe the two declarations and professions aforesaid, being thereunto required, shall be exempted from all the pains and penalties of all and every the aforementioned statutes made against popish recusants or Protestant nonconformists . . .

XIII. Provided always, and it is the true intent and meaning of this Act, that all the laws made and provided for the frequenting of divine service on the Lord's Day, commonly called Sunday, shall be still in force and executed against all persons that offend against the said laws, except such persons come to some congregation or assembly of religious worship allowed or permitted by this Act.

XIV. Provided always, and be it further enacted . . . that neither this Act nor any clause, article or thing herein contained shall extend or be construed to extend to give any ease, benefit or advantage to any papist or popish recusant whatsoever, or any person that shall deny in his preaching or writing the doctrine of the Blessed Trinity as it is declared in the aforesaid articles of religion . . .

Source: Andrew Browning (ed.), *English historical documents, 1660–1714*, London, 1953, pp. 402–03

7.2 Legislation to exclude Catholics from inheriting the throne

Part of the Act of Settlement, 1701

. . . whereas it hath been found by experience that it is inconsistent with the safety and welfare of this Protestant kingdom to be governed by a popish prince, or by any king or queen marrying a papist, the said Lords Spiritual and Temporal and Commons do further pray that it may be enacted, that all and every person and persons that is, are or shall be reconciled to or shall hold communion with the see or Church of Rome, or shall profess the popish religion, or shall marry a papist, shall be excluded and be for ever incapable to inherit, possess or enjoy the crown and government of this realm and Ireland and the dominions thereunto belonging or any part of the same, or to have, use or exercise any regal power, authority or jurisdiction within the same; and in all and every such case or cases the people of these realms shall be and are hereby absolved of their allegiance; and the said crown and government shall from time to time descend to and be enjoyed by such person or persons being Protestants as should have inherited and enjoyed the same in case the said person or persons so reconciled, holding communion or professing or marrying as aforesaid were naturally dead . . .

Source: Andrew Browning (ed.), *English historical documents, 1660–1714*, London, 1953, p. 127

7.3 Irish legislation against Catholics

Extracts from the Irish Act to prevent the further growth of popery, 1704

. . . be it enacted . . . that if any person or persons from and after the twenty-fourth day of March, in this present year of our Lord 1703, shall seduce, persuade or pervert any person or persons professing, or that shall profess, the protestant religion, to renounce, forsake, or adjure the same, and to profess the popish religion, or reconcile him or them to the church of Rome, then and in such case every such person or persons so seducing, as also every such protestant or protestants who shall be so seduced, perverted and reconciled to popery, shall for the said offenses, being thereof lawfully convicted, incur the danger and penalty of praemunire, mentioned in the statute of praemunire* made in England in the sixteenth year of the reign of king Richard the Second . . .

VI. And be it further enacted . . . that every papist, or person professing the popish religion, shall from and after the said twenty-fourth day of March be disabled, and is hereby made incapable, to buy and purchase either in his or in their own name, or in the name of any other person or persons to his or her use, or in trust for him or her, any manors, lands, tenements, or hereditaments,** or any rents or profits out of the same, or any leases or terms thereof, other than any term of years not exceeding thirty-one years, whereon a rent not less than two-thirds of the improved yearly value, at the time of the making such leases of the tenements leased, shall be reserved . . .

XV. Provided always, that no person shall take benefit by this act as a protestant within the intent and meaning hereof, that shall not conform to the church of Ireland as by the law established, and subscribe the declaration, and also take and subscribe the oath of adjuration following, viz. I A. B. do solemnly and sincerely, in the presence of God profess, testify and declare that I do believe, that in the sacrament of the Lord's Supper there is not any transubstantiation of the elements of bread and wine into the body and blood of Christ at or after the consecration thereof by any person whatsoever; and that the invocation or adoration of the Virgin Mary or any other saint and the sacrifice of the mass, as they are now used in the Church of Rome, are superstitious and idolatrous . . .

---

* see note on p. 14
** any inheritable property

Source: E. Curtis (ed.), *Irish historical documents*, 1172–1922, London, 1943, pp. 188–94

7.4 Scottish legislation in favour of Presbyterianism

Part of the Scottish Act for Securing the Protestant Religion and Presbyterian Church Government, 1707

. . . it being reasonable and necessary that the true Protestant religion, as presently professed within this kingdom with the worship, discipline and government of this church should be effectually and unalterably secured; therefore Her Majesty with advice and consent of the said estates of parliament doth hereby establish and confirm the said true Protestant religion and the worship, discipline and government of this church to continue without any alteration to the people of this land in all succeeding generations. And more especially Her Majesty with advice and consent foresaid ratifies, approves and forever confirms the fifth Act of the first parliament of King William and Queen Mary entitled Act Ratifying the Confession of Faith and settling Presbyterian Church Government, with all the other Acts of parliament relating thereto in prosecution of the Declaration of the Estates of this Kingdom containing the Claim of Right . . . And Her Majesty with advice and consent foresaid expressly provides and declares that the foresaid true Protestant religion contained in the above-mentioned Confession of Faith with the form and purity of worship presently in use within this church and its Presbyterian church government and discipline, that is to say, the government of the church by kirk sessions, presbyteries, provincial synods and general assemblies, all established by the foresaid Acts of parliament in accordance with the

Claim of Right shall remain and continue unalterable, and that the said Presbyterian government shall be the only government of the church within the kingdom of Scotland.

Source: W. C. Dickinson, *A source book of Scottish history to 1707*, vol. 3, London, 1954, pp. 489–90 [spelling modernised by the author]

Document case-study questions

The questions are based on the documents but you may need to look elsewhere in the book for relevant information.

1 How far does the Toleration Act of 1689 live up to nonconformist and Catholic expectations (7.1)?

2 What would be the impact of the legislation in 7.2 on Catholics?

3 Comment on the position of Catholics in Ireland after 1704. How far does the oath in this Act (7.3) reflect that required by the 1678 Test Act in England (6.5)?

4 What was the reason for this legislation in favour of Presbyterian government in Scotland (7.4)?

Select bibliography

General reading

As an introduction, see S. Doran and C. Durston, *Princes, pastors and people: the church and religion in England 1529–1689*, London, 1991, which charts the religious changes in the period covered by this book. For the Catholics in particular, J. Bossy, *The English Catholic community*, London, 1973, remains essential reading. Of the extensive work on the Puritans, C. Durston and J. Eales (eds.), *The culture of English Puritanism*, Basingstoke, 1996, considers some of the most important aspects of Puritanism as a religious culture, while W. Lamont, *Puritanism and historical controversy*, London, 1996, is the latest addition to the debate about the role and significance of Puritanism.

The reign of Elizabeth

D. MacCulloch, *Building a godly realm: the establishment of English Protestantism 1558–1603*, London, 1992, is a short pamphlet which addresses the social and political impact of English Protestantism in the reign of Elizabeth. P. Collinson, *Godly people*, London, 1983, is a collection of essays about the second and third generation of Protestants. In *The birthpangs of Protestant England*, London, 1988, he demonstrates how the English Reformation was more than a simple change in religious belief and had much wider implications for sixteenth- and seventeenth-century England. The Catholics are less well served for this period but D. Rosman, *From Catholic to Protestant*, London, 1996, explores the role of religion in people's lives, including the continued appeal of Catholicism.

Early Stuart England

An excellent study of religion in early Stuart England is K. Fincham, *The early Stuart church*, Basingstoke, 1993. For the fortunes of the Catholics, see P. Lake, 'Anti-popery: the structure of a prejudice' in R. Cust and A. Hughes (eds.), *Conflict in early Stuart England*, London, 1989. C. Russell, *The causes of the English Civil War*, Oxford, 1990, analyses the problem of competing theologies within the two (or even three) state churches and is essential reading. More specifically, Julian Davies, *The Caroline captivity of the church: Charles I and the remoulding of Anglicanism, 1625–1641*, Oxford, 1992, is a recent examination of the church in the reign of Charles I.

The Civil War years and the Interregnum

J. Morrill, 'The impact of Puritanism' in J. Morrill (ed.), *The impact of the English Civil War*, London, 1991, examines the energetic efforts of the Puritans during the Civil War to effect a Godly Revolution, while his essay 'The church in England 1642–9' in J. Morrill (ed.), *Reactions to the English Civil War*, London, 1982, shows the extent of resistance to their ambitions. The failed hopes of the Puritans in the 1650s is clearly demonstrated in A. Hughes, 'The frustrations of the godly' in J. Morrill (ed.), *Revolution and Restoration: England in the 1650s*, London, 1992. A useful introduction to the Levellers, followed by an extensive collection of Leveller writings, can be found in G. Aylmer, *The Levellers and the English Revolution*, London, 1975. There is abundant literature on Oliver Cromwell, for example, B. Coward, *Oliver Cromwell*, London, 1991.

The Restoration and beyond

The work of T. Harris, P. Seaward and M. Goldie (eds.), *The politics of religion in Restoration England*, Oxford, 1990, challenges the traditional view that religious passion was a spent force in the Restoration period. P. Seaward, *The Restoration, 1660–1688*, Basingstoke, 1991, especially the chapter 'Conflicts of conscience', demonstrates how much of the heat in Restoration politics was generated by religious argument. For the distinction between Catholicism and popery in the minds of the English, see J. Miller, *Popery and politics in England 1660–1688*, Cambridge, 1973, which shows how the one was generally tolerated while the other was the object of fear and hatred.

Scotland

G. Donaldson, *Scottish church history*, Edinburgh, 1985, is a selection of writings about the Scottish church from its beginnings, but the majority of the work concentrates on the Scottish Reformation. M. Lynch, *Scotland: a new history*, London, 1991, is a comprehensive history of Scotland which pays due regard to religion throughout. More detailed studies can be found in the excellent J. Wormald (ed.), *Scotland revisited*, London, 1991, especially J. Kirk, 'Reformation and revolution, kirk and crown 1560–1690', and A. I. Macinnes, 'Covenanting, revolution and municipal enterprise'.

Ireland

Work specifically on Irish church history for this period is less easy to identify. Useful essays can be found in T. W. Moody and F. X. Martin (eds.), *The course of Irish history*, Cork, 1967; for example: A. Clarke, 'The colonization of Ulster and the rebellion of 1641', and J. G. Simm, 'The Restoration and the Jacobite war (1660–91)'. See also, J. Fulton, *The tragedy of belief: division, politics and religion in Ireland*, Oxford, 1991, especially, 'Anglo-Irish ascendancy, Protestant subordination, and Catholic oppression: Ireland, 1600–1800'.

Glossary

Arminian	critic of Calvinist predestination theology
church-papist	Roman Catholic who attended the Protestant church
Convocation	general assembly of the clergy which met at the same time as parliament
Covenanter	signatory of the National Covenant (Scotland)
crypto-Catholic	secretly Catholic
Digger	member of a group which developed ideas of a communist Utopia
dissenter	a person who refused to submit to the episcopal church of the Reformation
episcopacy	church government by bishops
episcopal	advocating church government by bishops
episcopalian	a person who belonged to a church governed by bishops
Fifth Monarchist	zealot who believed in the imminent second coming of Christ, who would establish a government by the saints
Jesuit	member of the Society of Jesus, which was founded to counter Protestantism through missionary work
Leveller	member of a radical sect committed to the abolition of social distinctions and religious persecution
nonconformist	a person within the Church of England who declined to conform to certain practices prescribed by the 1559 Prayer Book
Papist	Roman Catholic
prophesying	meeting to discuss scripture, usually in front of a lay audience
Puritan	one who wished further to reform the Church of England
recusant	non-attender at state church, usually a Roman Catholic
sabbatarianism	keeping Sunday holy by restricting all activities to those of a religious nature
separatist	a person who repudiated the ordinances and discipline of the established church and met in secret in the reigns of Elizabeth, James I and Charles I

Chronology

1529 Opening of Reformation Parliament

1534 Act of Supremacy: Henry VIII acknowledged as 'Protector and Supreme Head of the English Church'

1536–37 Irish parliament enacts legislation of English Reformation Parliament

1542 Mary Stuart becomes queen of Scotland

1547 Henry VIII dies
Accession of Edward VI
Chantries Act

1549 First Edwardian Prayer Book, or Book of Common Prayer, issued
First Act of Uniformity

1552 Second Edwardian Prayer Book, or Book of Common Prayer, issued
Second Act of Uniformity

1553 Forty-Two Articles issued
Edward VI dies
Accession of Mary Tudor

1554 Act of Repeal
England reunited with Rome

1554 Mary Tudor marries Philip II of Spain

1557 'First Band of the Lords of the Congregation of Christ' established in Scotland

1558 Mary Tudor dies
Accession of Elizabeth
Elizabethan Prayer Book issued

1559 Treaty of Cateau-Cambrésis
Severe treatment of French Huguenots
Acts of Supremacy and Uniformity
Deprivation of Marian (Roman Catholic) bishops

1560 Publication of the Geneva Bible in English
Lords of the Congregation (leading Protestant Scottish nobles) sign Treaty of Berwick with England
Treaty of Edinburgh
Scottish Reformation Parliament

1561 Mary, queen of Scots, returns to Scotland

1563 Convocation approves the Thirty-Nine Articles

1564 Dispute over clerical dress (Vestments Controversy)

1565   *Book of Advertisements* issued to address the question of uniformity in the rites and ceremonies of church

1567   Mary, queen of Scots, abdicates
        Mary's son crowned James VI of Scotland
        Mary seeks refuge in England
        Revolt in Spanish Netherlands (Low Countries)

1568   Roman Catholic seminary founded at Douai

1569   Rebellion in the North

1570   Pope Pius V publishes the Bull *Regnans in Excelsis* which excommunicated Elizabeth
        Thomas Cartwright lectures in favour of Presbyterianism at Cambridge University

1571   Ridolfi Plot discovered
        Confirmation by statute of the Thirty-Nine Articles

1572   Andrew Melville returns to Scotland from Geneva

1574   Arrival in England of the first missionary priests

1575   Edmund Grindal becomes archbishop of Canterbury

1577   Grindal suspended for his defiance over suppressing prophesyings

1580   First Irish rebellion fails (1580–83)
        First Jesuit missionaries arrive in England

1581   Act to retain the Queen's Majesty's Subjects in due obedience (i.e. recusancy law)

1583   John Whitgift becomes archbishop of Canterbury upon the death of Grindal
        Throckmorton Plot discovered

1584   Scottish parliament passes 'Black Acts' against Presbyterianism

1585   Act against Jesuits, Seminary Priests and like disobedient persons (i.e. recusancy law)
        English troops arrive in the Low Countries

1586   Babington Plot discovered

1587   Mary, queen of Scots, executed

1588   Spanish Armada
        Marprelate Letters published

1589   Protestant Henri of Navarre becomes king of France (Henri IV) and converts to Catholicism
        England lends support to France in the face of Spanish threats

1591   Trial and imprisonment of Presbyterian leaders

1593   John Penry and other Protestant separatist leaders executed

1594   Nine Years War in Ireland begins

1598   Henri IV of France issues Edict of Nantes

1603   Nine Years War ends
        Elizabeth dies
        Accession of James I
        Millenary Petition presented to James

1604   Hampton Court Conference
        New ecclesiastical canons issued
        Richard Bancroft becomes archbishop of Canterbury

1605 Puritan petitioning campaign culminates in the Northamptonshire petition
Gunpowder Plot

1611 George Abbot becomes archbishop of Canterbury
Authorised Bible published

1613 James's daughter Elizabeth marries Frederick V of the Palatinate

1617 James visits Scotland

1618 *Book of Sports* issued
Thirty Years War begins
Five Articles of Perth

1619 Synod of Dort

1621 William Laud translated to bishopric of St David's

1625 James I dies
Accession of Charles I
William Laud chosen to preach before parliamentary session
Appointment of Arminian Richard Montagu as royal chaplain

1626 York House Conference

1629 House of Commons passes resolution against religious innovations (i.e. Arminianism)
Beginning of Charles I's Personal Rule

1632 Thomas Wentworth appointed Lord Deputy in Ireland

1633 Charles visits Scotland and later decides to introduce a new Prayer Book in Scotland
William Laud translated to archbishopric of Canterbury
Book of Sports reissued

1635 Ecclesiastical canons, based on those of 1604, issued in Scotland

1637 John Bastwicke, Henry Burton and William Prynne mutilated
New Prayer Book imposed on Scots provoking riot in St Giles's church, Edinburgh
Elections to National Assembly in Scotland

1638 A National Covenant drawn up to abolish the Prayer Book in Scotland
Scottish National Assembly abolishes bishops

1639 First Bishops' War

1640 Short Parliament meets and is dissolved
New canons issued by Convocation
Second Bishops' War
Long Parliament meets
New canons condemned
Laud imprisoned
'Root and Branch' petition against bishops presented to parliament

1641 Wentworth executed
'Root and Branch' bill for the abolition of bishops presented to parliament
King Charles visits Scotland and makes concessions to the Covenanters
Allegations of a Royalist plot – the 'Incident' – against the Covenanter leaders
Irish rebellion

1642 Act excluding bishops from parliament passed
Civil War begins
Parliament closes theatres in London
Confederation of Kilkenny (provisional Catholic government) set up in Ireland

1643 Westminster Assembly of Divines meets to discuss new church settlement
Scots agree to Solemn League and Covenant

1644 Rifts between religious Presbyterians and religious Independents in Westminster Assembly

1645 Use of Book of Common Prayer banned
Laud executed

1646 King Charles surrenders to the Scots
Parliament passes an ordinance establishing a national Presbyterian church
Parliament abolishes episcopate

1647 Levellers produce Agreement of the People and infiltrate army ranks
Alliance between King Charles and the Scots (the Engagement)

1648 Second Civil War
Thirty Years War ends

1649 Trial and execution of Charles I
Start of 11-year Interregnum
Treaty of Kilkenny
Declaration of English republic
Massacres of Catholics at Drogheda and Wexford, Ireland

1650 Act for the propagation of the gospel in Wales
Blasphemy Act
Repeal of the Act of Uniformity

1653 Oliver Cromwell appointed Lord Protector

1655 Appointment of the major-generals as moral guardians

1658 Oliver Cromwell dies

1660 Declaration of Breda
Charles II proclaimed king
Scottish parliament passes Act of Recissory annulling all legislation since 1633, restoring the bishops and forbidding conventicles
Worcester House Conference to address the future of the church; Worcester House Declaration

1661 First meeting of Cavalier Parliament
Restoration of bishops to the House of Lords
Corporation Act
Return of church courts
Act of Settlement in Ireland

1662 Convocation revises Prayer Book
Act of Uniformity
Remonstrance drawn up in Ireland
King Charles's first Declaration of Indulgence

1663 First Declaration of Indulgence withdrawn

1664 First Conventicles Act

1665 Act of Explanation in Ireland
Five Mile Act

1666 Pentland Rising in Scotland

1670 Second Conventicles Acts in both England and Scotland
Treaty of Dover

1672 King Charles issues second Declaration of Indulgence

1673 Second Declaration of Indulgence cancelled
First Test Act passed
James, duke of York, openly a Catholic

1677 William Sancroft appointed archbishop of Canterbury

1678 Popish Plot and first executions of alleged plotters
Second Test Act

1679 Meeting of first Exclusion Parliament

1681 Defeat for exclusion

1685 King Charles II dies
Accession of King James II

1687 King James issues first Declaration of Indulgence
King attempts to have Test and Corporation Acts repealed

1688 King James issues second Declaration of Indulgence
Arrest of William Sancroft and six bishops for refusing to publish the Declaration
Invasion of England by William of Orange
King James flees

1689 Accession of King William III and Queen Mary II (the Glorious Revolution)
Toleration Act passed

1690 General Assembly of the Kirk re-establishes the Presbyterian church in Scotland
Battle of the Boyne

1691 Treaty of Limerick, Ireland

1692 Irish (Dublin) parliament meets

1694 Queen Mary dies

1701 Act of Settlement

1702 King William dies
Accession of Queen Anne
Tory demands for an Occasional Conformity Act

1707 Act of Union of England and Scotland
Scottish kirk secures guarantees for Presbyterianism in the Act of Union

1709 Dr Henry Sacheverell's sermon questioning the basis of the Glorious Revolution

1711 Occasional Conformity Act passed

1712 Scottish Toleration Act in favour of episcopalianism

1714 Queen Anne dies
Accession of Lutheran King George I

Index

Index

Millenarian Utopianism, 57
Millenary Petition (1603), 28
monasteries, dissolution of the, 2, 20
Montagu, Richard, 33–4, 37
moral control, Puritans as agents of, 58–9, 61

Netherlands, *see* Low Countries
New gag for an old goose, A, 33–4
Nine Years War (1594), 18
nonconformists, *see* dissenters
Northamptonshire petition (1605), 29, 35
Northern Rising (1569), 12, 22

Oates, Titus, 65, 66

Palatinate, and foreign policy, 31–2, 44–5
Parker, Matthew, archbishop of Canterbury, 6, 8, 10
parliament: Cavalier Parliament, 62–3; and Charles I, 38–9, 45; and the Civil War, 50–1, 51–2, 54, 55–6
Penn, William, 64
Pentland Rising (1666), 68
Philip II, king of Spain, 3, 12, 17, 21, 22, 23
popish plot (1678), 65, 66
predestination, doctrine of, 3, 8, 28; and Arminianism, 32, 33, 37, 38; and Puritanism, 58
Presbyterianism: and the Civil War, 51–2, 55–6; and the Elizabethan church, 8, 11, 12; in Ireland, 43, 54, 69, 77; and the Restoration settlement, 62, 63, 68, 69; in Scotland, 19–20, 27–8, 30–1, 68, 70, 76, 80–1; *see also* Puritans
'prophesyings', Puritan, 8, 11
Protestantism: and the Civil War, 54–6; and the Elizabethan church, 8–9, 12; Englishness equated with, 3, 12; in France (Huguenots), 20, 21, 24, 77, 78; and the Glorious Revolution, 74–5; in Ireland, 4–5, 17–18, 43, 52–4, 68–70, 77; *see also* Presbyterianism; Puritans; Reformation
Prynne, William, 40–1
Puritans: and the Caroline church, 37, 38–41, 45–7; and the Elizabethan church, 8–9, 10–12; and the Glorious Revolution, 74; godly magistrates, 24, 28, 30, 41; and the Interregnum, 58–9; and the Jacobean church, 27, 28–9, 30, 33, 34–5, 77–8; Northamptonshire petition (1605), 29, 35; and princely authority, 24; and the 'Root and Branch' petition, 45, 46, 48–9; *see also* Presbyterianism
Pym, John, 38, 53, 54

Quakers, 63, 64

radicalism, and the Interregnum, 56–8

recusancy laws/fines, 10, 13–14, 30, 42, 67, 78
Reformation: in Continental Europe, 1; Edwardian, 1, 2–3, 4–5; Henrician, 1–2; in Scotland, 5, 18–20
Reformation Parliament, 1
Restoration, 62–73; and Catholics, 64–5; Clarendon Code, 62–3, 64; and dissenters, 63–4
Ridolfi Plot (1571), 12, 22
Roman Catholic Church, *see* Catholicism
'Root and Branch' petition, 45, 46, 48–9

Sabbatarian Movement, 28
Sacheverell, Dr Henry, 75
Sancroft, William, archbishop of Canterbury, 67
Scotland: and Charles I, 42–3, 45, 50, 54–5, 76; and Charles II, 52, 68; and the Civil War, 50, 51–2, 54–5; Confession of Faith, 25; and the Glorious Revolution, 76; and James II and VII, 68, 76; and James VI, 19–20, 27–8, 30, 30–1; National Covenant (Covenanters), 43, 47–8, 50, 51, 52, 54; Presbyterian church government, 19–20, 27–8, 70, 80–1; Protestant Reformation in, 5, 18–20
Seven Bishops' Case, 67
Somerset, duke of, Lord Protector, 2
Spain: and Elizabethan foreign policy, 17, 18, 21–3; and Jacobean foreign policy, 29, 30, 31, 32
Spanish Armada (1588), 22, 41

Tenison, Thomas, archbishop of Canterbury, 75
Thirty Years War (1618–48), 31–2, 34
Thirty-Nine Articles of Religion, 8, 29, 38, 43
Tillotson, John, archbishop of Canterbury, 75
Tories, 65, 67
trade and industry, and religious minorities, 78
transubstantiation, doctrine of, 7
Trent, Council of, 3
Tyconnel, earl of, Lord Lieutenant of Ireland, 69

United (Dutch) Provinces, 23

Wentworth, Thomas, Lord Deputy of Ireland, 43, 52, 53, 54
Westminster Assembly of Divines, 55–6
Whigs, 65, 66
Whitgift, John, archbishop of Canterbury, 8, 11
William III, King (William of Orange), 64, 67, 68, 75, 76; and Ireland, 69–70, 77
Winstanley, Gerrard, 58
Worcester House Declaration, 62

York House conference (1626), 37–8